CIPRIAN BADESCU studied business and sociology, obtaining a doctorate in sociology of organizations, followed by a post-doctorate in sociology of culture, cultural economy, and social economics at the Romanian Academy. The two major themes of economy and sociology have formed the basis of much of his work, such as his 2013 book *Fundamentele culturale ale crizelor economice: de la etnoeconomie la teoria proprietății identitare (Cultural Foundations of Economic Crises. From Ethnoeconomy to the Theory of Identity Property)*. His more recent work includes participating in a two-year research project on improving research infrastructure on social assistance in low- and middle-income countries, completed at the Global Development Institute, University of Manchester.

Published by
Pɜrtınənt Press
an imprint of
Oxford Legal Publishing Limited
www.thepertinentpress.co.uk
OXFORD

"Publishers of Intelligent Books" © 2017

PɜRTINƎNT PRESS
focuses on and aims to further study and knowledge in
philosophy, history, cultural studies, and theology.

PɜRTINƎNT PRESS™
is a registered trademark

Published in the United Kingdom by Oxford Legal Publishing Limited
© 2020 by Oxford Legal Publishing Limited

British Library Cataloguing in Publication Data
Data Available

Oxford Legal Publishing Limited
is registered in England as No. 10898419
at the following address:
52 Cornmarket Street
Oxford OX1 3HJ

ISBN: 978-1-912142-26-2

Ciprian I Badescu

'WELFARE CAPITALISM' AND THE REGIONAL WORLDS

REFLECTIONS ON THE FOURTH CAPITALISM

Foreword by Prof. Catalin Zamfir

P3RTINƏNT PRESS

OXFORD

To my family.

CONTENTS

ACKNOWLEDGEMENTS

I am especially indebted to Prof. Armando Barrientos who has been supportive of my career goals, facilitating my participation in the project 'Improving research infrastructure on social assistance' under the aegis of the Global Development Institute, University of Manchester.

I am grateful to Prof. Cătălin Zamfir for his advice and support throughout my time as a PhD student and researcher at the Institute for Quality of Life, the Romanian Academy.

I would especially like to thank Prof. Martin Powell and Prof. Iestyn Williams for their input during the initial phase of my research endeavour. I am thankful to Rachel Posaner, Emma Green and all of those who advised and supported me on the research journey I have taken during my collaboration with the Health Services Management Centre, University of Birmingham.

Nobody has been more important than my family. I wish to thank my loving and supportive wife, Alina, and my two wonderful daughters, Teodora and Ana-Maria, who provide an unending wellspring of inspiration.

Ciprian Badescu

LIST OF ILLUSTRATIONS

Tables

Diagrams

Figures

FOREWORD

A BOOK ON THE RELATIONSHIP BETWEEN WELFARE CAPITALISM AND regional worlds reveals new insights into the study of welfare state developments. As this book unveils, the author's approach evolves from being a synthesis of comparative literature on welfare regimes to still unexplored 'worlds' of welfare regimes. The debate surrounding the problems of welfare regimes has been heavily slanted towards the number and the composition of such 'worlds' of welfare regimes, missing the imperative of considering a glocalized world whose extension becomes intelligible only by a multimodal comparison. The existing literature is marked by incongruence in terms of theoretical and empirical findings.

Ciprian Badescu has aptly reviewed the literature on welfare state developments, revealing the 'real type' configurations.

The literature on the comparative welfare state developments is deeply rooted in the tradition established by Esping-Andersen's seminal work: *The Three Worlds of Welfare Capitalism*. Esping-Andersen's perspective focuses on explaining the differences between welfare states based on a threefold typology. The modal conclusion is that there are three ideal types of welfare regimes as originated in Esping-Andersen's model of the 'Three Worlds'.

The challenging issue is to establish a multimodal perspective on welfare regimes. The author starts from such a basic assumption that the world of welfare regimes is rooted in a multi-polar dimensionality.

As a matter of fact, the author argues the worlds of welfare regimes are more than three. The 'lens' needs to be changed. There is not only one modal conclusion: globality is not the only explanatory factor. There is also a regionality within globality which cannot be ignored. Regional worlds make the globality itself more 'eligible'. Capitalism has developed itself in time through a series of successive and co-existent processes of releasing and capturing wealth.

In order to build a more comprehensive approach to this process, Ciprian Badescu proceeds by revisiting J. Lampert's theory on the essence of capitalism (2006). In Lampert's view, 'wealth has to break away from ruling functionaries and attach itself to fluid labour, liquid investments, and unchartered markets' (Ibid, p. 162). Such 'break away' processes allow for capitalism to intrinsically exist in a rather 'regional style', regardless of its global manifestation.

The literature is still skimming around the edges. Comprehending the problematic of welfare state developments requires remodelling not only the welfare state, but also its theoretical and empirical foundations. This book signals the imperative of a new normativity with regional 'worlds' taking centre stage.

Catalin Zamfir
Director of Research Institute for Quality of Life
Romanian Academy

'WELFARE CAPITALISM' AND THE REGIONAL WORLDS

REFLECTIONS ON THE FOURTH CAPITALISM

PART I
'MULTIPLE GLOBALIZATION'
AND
'WELFARE CAPITALISM'

WHY I WROTE THIS BOOK

GLOBALIZATION STUDIES COVERS THE AGENDA FOR A GROWING number of sociologists. As Immanuel Wallerstein argues, the fact that social science has focused so monotonously in the last few decades on globalization has induced an effect which can properly be assimilated to a kind of epistemological emaciation. This depletion has usually been balanced by a certain diversification of theoretical directions within yet the same globalist paradigm. The most significant examples include the theory of multiple globalizations espoused by sociologists (see Aman, 1998; Appadurai, 1996; Bonilla, 1998) – and Saskia Sassen's new theoretical approach focusing on the 'scalar analytics' and on the theory of 'scaling the global' (Sassen, 2003; 2008). Sassen makes a distinction between two sets of globalizing processes: those which occur at the global scale (for instance, the emergence of international institutions etc.) and those that evolve at the local or national scale, yet denote a global meaning themselves. Their conjoining feature is that all these types of globalizing processes involve or induce 'trans-boundary networks and formations'.

The denotative feature of the second set of globalizing processes is what Sassen called the 'particular scaling of the global' (2003). This phenomenon has also been called 'ethno-globalization' (Badescu, 2008), a definition which focuses on the power of nations to individually remodel the globalizing processes or even to initiate global vectors by themselves. One relevant example of ethno-globalization is the global trend of the rise of nationality throughout the 19th and 20th centuries. The *national pattern* has preserved its local character and there are a lot of processes largely relevant for national scaling of the global. Unlike Sassen's conclusions, our hypothesis is that national scaling has a self-reinforcing effect, so that its intervening in the globalization process comes to modify even the pattern of this process. Therefore, the relationship between national and global needs additional clarifications from those two opposite directions. Interference of national in globalization process is much more than merely a scaling effect on the global. Inversely, the globalizing effect is hardly a systematic one being that its side effects seem to be for the most part destructive and debilitating (at least for an intermediate period but with no less severe long-term effects). This requires a new approach to the relationship between national and global, to correctly decode what is meant by both terms.

Nationality as a *pattern of collective organization* appears to be a global scale phenomenon while it continues to preserve its character and content no matter the orientation and practices of the local elites. The affirmation of nationality at the global scale did not annul its content, so we can consider this as both a global and local pattern and an example of processes illustrating the 'particular scaling of global'. I call this phenomenon 'co-existential globalization' - to be balanced against 'hegemonic globalization' (cf. Badescu, I. and Badescu, I. C. 2014). Therefore, we may comprehend a possible distinction between the proper *globalization* and the *global scale phenomena*. I include in this category, any *specific global pattern,* preserving its specific character and content despite its global span. Such a pattern is a global-scale one, but it nevertheless preserves its specific character.

The quest for welfare is a phenomenon bearing a multi-scalar manifestation and calls for a renovated debate. There is scattered literature on welfare realities in both the developed and the developing worlds. In the 1990s, welfare theory developments arrived at a critical theoretical juncture, and Abrahamson (1999) identified a substantial increase in the use of welfare state typologies in this decade. Gough (2008) identified two methodological directions that have predominated the 'welfare modelling business' (Abrahamson, 1999). The first comprises a historical and institutional perspective (cf. Inglot (2008), Heclo (1974) and Weir, Orloff and Skocpol (1988). The second consists of comparative analysis heavily slanted towards classifying welfare regimes. Gosta Esping-Andersen's seminal work on welfare capitalism (1990) marked the debut of a renovated 'comparative social policy research' (Powell, M., Barrientos, A., 2015). He focused his analysis on 18 OECD countries,[1] 'employing regression analysis in the context of linking policy and politics' (Barrientos, A., 2014). In recent years, the Mediterranean group of welfare states (Italy, Spain, Portugal and Greece) has been added (Castles 1998). The developed 'world' of welfare regimes has been favoured, with developing countries such as those from the Central and Eastern European area[2] still not fitting the Eurocentric world view. Nevertheless, the theoretical discourse on welfare realities has been marked by incompleteness in terms of 'composition, and number, of welfare state regimes' (Bambra, 2007). The two methodologies identified by Gough (2008) point to an incongruence regarding the methodological directions developed in the literature.

Moreover, in the 1990s, developments in welfare theory were infused with ideas of globalization, signalling attempts to harmonize the socio-economic discourse. I. Gough (2008) noticed a 'complementarity between labour markets and welfare systems' as a particularity of

---

1   This area comprises the 'Central and Eastern European Countries (CEECs) [which] is an OECD term for the group of countries comprising Albania, Bulgaria, Croatia, the Czech Republic, Hungary, Poland, Romania, the Slovak Republic, Slovenia, and the three Baltic States: Estonia, Latvia and Lithuania.' (Source Publication: 'Agricultural Policies in OECD Countries: Monitoring and Evaluation 2000: Glossary of Agricultural Policy Terms', OECD, https://stats.oecd.org/glossary/detail.asp?ID=303)

2   Australia, United States, New Zealand, Canada, Ireland, United Kingdom, Italy, Japan, France, Germany, Finland, Switzerland, Austria, Belgium, Netherlands, Denmark, Norway, Sweden.

Keynesian welfare states. Globalization brought to bear specific global patterns, marking the debut of a multi-scalar manifestation of politics and policy. Gough (2008, p. 53) argues that 'this harmony between economy and social policy is commonly perceived to have broken down with the challenge of monetarism in the 1970s' although complementary voices (cf. Sassen, 2003) brought into debate the idea of multi-scalar globalization processes. Globalization is manifested in a dynamic, multi-scalar perspective, with both national and global patterns.

The aims of this book are twofold. First, it completes a systematic review of welfare state regimes theories starting with the tradition established by Esping-Andersen (1990). Second, the book opens up an additional line of interpretation based on the third type of capitalism (whose main instrument of expansion remains transnationals combined with the state but acting in a highly complex world configuration which is also dealing with a 'regionalized world order' (Higgott, T., 2016)).

My idea is that in this phase of global expansion of capitalism, its instruments (i.e. transnationals) are not interested in supporting the welfare regimes in a universal style, but in a regional one. Capital is forced to accept regional differences and sometimes even national differences. It is in the interest of capital's expansion to value all sorts of differences because a very important factor of growth in the postmodern era is the differential rent or what the theorists of firm calls 'quasi-rent'.

Capitalism subsists historically only if it is capable of creating factors of its internal differentiation. In default of a creative power, capitalism fails. Basically, such a failure does not affect the system itself but its evolutionary form. Our applied study refers mainly to the arrival of the fourth capitalism. To enlighten this issue, we first need to shed light upon another issue – namely, the rise and decline of each historical type of capitalism. The conclusion of this research's investigation is that there are four types of historical capitalism, with humanity already having entered the fourth age of capitalism. Capitalism has the power to create factors of differentiation alongside its historic evolution, although these factors are competitive and often conflicting. I submit that a certain type of evolutionary capitalism has never ever vanished completely but has survived on as a paradigm, that is, it has persisted as a paradigmatic formula in the mind of capitalists and of strategists of capitalism, hence supporting regional conflicting capitalist systems. As a matter of fact, each type of historical capitalism has contributed to filtering *patterns of capitalism* that can be perpetuated as *paradigmatic formulas of doing business*.

Regional worlds are the main consequence of the new phase of capital expansion in the global era. Therefore, I thought it to be helpful to revisit the welfare state theories, revealing a third type of capitalism, different from the previous two based on the strategy of the world's homogenization and not its differentiation. Capitalism is able to encompass a world economy and different regional business networks but it cannot and is not interested in homogenizing the world itself, as the main factor of local prosperity is quasi-rent, i.e., the rent of regional identity (of what the new global theories used to call glocalization phenomenon).

Thus, it has become imperative to revisit the large number of welfare state theories starting with Esping-Andersen's three ideal 'worlds' of the welfare regimes but going further. Esping-Andersen's analysis results from considering that capital is the single factor of postmodern expansion and globalization induces three welfare regimes because capital's prevalence in the relationship between the state and capital presumes such a conclusion.

There is still a large theoretical debate in the comparative literature explaining the development of the welfare state (cf. Powell, M., 2015), entailing a rather explanatory framework for what has now become a 'welfare modelling business' (Abrahamson, 1999). It could signal elements of Kuhnian normal science (cf. Van Kersbergen, K., Vis, B., 2015), preventing the emergence of scientific endeavour in terms of new theoretical and methodological developments.

How can we overcome the shortfall of being bogged down in an explanatory framework reflected in almost 30 years of modelling business in the welfare literature? *The Three Worlds* gained traction with academia, although Esping-Andersen's typology 'is at risk of becoming an, what me might call, unproductive intellectual straitjacket standing in the way of, rather than being helpful for, asking theoretically interesting questions about the welfare state.' (Van Kersbergen, K., Vis, B., 2015, p. 2).

Therefore, the affirmation of an epistemic community focused on learning new perspectives on the study of welfare realities needs a new discourse. My own perspective is that in the postmodern era, the new capitalist expansion appears to be determined by two factors: a) capital itself, whose expansion takes on the form of globalization (i.e., becoming a single world system), and b) multiple regional worlds, rooted in such a specific set of conditions that no capitalist forces could homogenize them, nor would they be interested in doing so, just because it is a source of value added called quasi-rent.

Part I of the book is dedicated entirely to a renovated approach to welfare state theories, models, concepts and types. Special emphasis will be laid on the conceptual and methodological aspects regarding the theoretical constructions of types, models, theoretical frames of welfare regimes throughout different national, regional and even continental areas. The welfare-related issues are analysed by economists as well as by sociologists: welfare economics tries to evaluate well-being from an economic perspective, invoking mechanisms and parameters belonging to the economic understanding of modern society.

Part II is dedicated to an examination of the relations between welfare state and 'regional worlds'. as they are modelled either by the effects of globalization or because of the welfare conditions that make migration more possible. Issues like the *corridors of remittances* or the concept of *cross-border networks* facilitate a better understanding of the phenomena, shedding a light on issues like migration and its corresponding parameters (e.g. remittances, net migration) entailing new socio-spatial configurations. The remittance corridors create not only the new *welfare cores* but also new types of social, economic and money polarization. Migrants' social corridors re-embed a country in *a new welfare area* or region.

Part III is dedicated to the 'fourth capitalism' which is an unexpected illustration of a *coincidentia oppositorum,* as such a capitalism is not driven only by the quest for profit but the community involved in the quest for welfare. The tensions between profit and welfare, capitalists and communities, states and corporations, market and family etc. claim a new pattern of negotiation and new arrangements that announce a new capitalism which, historically considered, is the *fourth capitalism*.

To study welfare capitalism in relation to the regional worlds equates with a response to the challenging issue of what is meant by:

> [Knowledge] management, that, on its turn, is open to multiple epistemologies, which gives access to alternative types of knowledge worlds: possible worlds, plausible worlds, probable worlds and actual worlds. Knowledge-bearing agents use their knowledge in this world to take actions' that lead to welfare state melioration in a designedly regional world.[3]

The regional worlds act upon knowledge development as a set of constraints which, on their turn, influences the research endeavour on welfare state developments. The epistemological challenge of such a regional differentiation is to find out the adequate path which allows us to get the final assurance that what we belief of a regional welfare regime is at the same time justified and true. Such a purpose asks for a special approach on what we may call the *epistemic welfare modelling business* as an assessment:

> [Not] in terms of answering questions to which they give priority but in relation to questions that they would see as important if they absorbed parts of the available public knowledge of which they are currently ignorant. (Kitcher, P., 2006, p. 61)

To reach a new synthesis of welfare regimes studies requires a cross-borders approach which, on its turn, asks for a deep and integrative analysis of the methodological and epistemological aspects of regional welfare regimes studies. The knowledge of regional welfare regimes unveils what we may call the 'epistemic welfare' 'worlds' that equate with regional

---

3   Boisot, M., & MacMillan, I. (2004). Crossing Epistemological Boundaries: Managerial and Entrepreneurial Approaches to Knowledge Management. Long Range Planning, 37 (6), 505-524. http://dx.doi.org/10.1016/j.lrp.2004.09.002

constraints of a triple nature: subjective, objective and methodological. There are multiple differences issuing from what people believe of their own welfare state, what are objectively regional welfare regimes and what scientists advance regarding the actual knowledge of welfare state in a given regional world, based on different methods, typologies and theoretical models. Therefore, theories of welfare regimes need a multi-stage holistic approach of all these aspects of knowledge development in different regional worlds and throughout a hypothetically single integrated world, modelled by what Esping-Andersen called the 'three worlds of welfare capitalism' (1990).

Over the last three decades there has been a steady increase in the literature on the relations between capitalism and welfare state. Social quest of welfare at the global scale has transformed capitalism, leading to the consecrated syntagma of 'welfare capitalism'. Esping-Andersen's threefold classification ('liberal', 'corporatist' and 'social democratic') (1990) has become a cornerstone in comparative welfare state research. The quest for a path towards a 'good society' (cf. Zamfir, C., 2013) (that is, the quest for welfare), beyond the market, in a mix with the quest for profit, leads to a social reconstruction of the capitalist system itself. I opted to call such a new social construction *the fourth capitalism*. The market unveiled its inability to secure general access to welfare provision, so people had to look for a complementary path towards a good society and, therefore, towards a welfare state. If we want to understand this type of evolutionary capitalism, we need to readjust the classical theoretical thesis of capitalism based on reconsidering the impact of the welfare 'regional worlds' upon the global capitalism.

Esping-Andersen's concept of welfare regime requires a new analytical approach that allows us to consider the huge diversity of situations depending on so many differences regarding:

> [...] the institutional arrangements, rules and understandings that guide and shape concurrent social policy decisions, expenditure developments, problem definitions, and even the respond-and-demand structure of citizens and welfare consumers. The existence of policy

regimes reflects the circumstance that short-term policies, reforms, debates, and decision-making take place within frameworks of historical institutionalization that differ qualitatively between countries. (Esping-Andersen, G., 1990, p. 80)

Even starting analysis based exclusively on Esping-Andersen's concept, we are requested to make a distinction between three types of welfare worlds each depending on its own welfare regime.

Hence, we have to revisit welfare theories as we take into account the fact that the relation between capital and welfare (i.e. the relation between capital and communities) induces differentiation of regional worlds that by feedback compel the system to adopt different regional and even national strategies under the same purpose: getting the added value.

Consequently, I developed Esping-Andersen's approach employing a new idea and a new conception of globalization, entailing a dualist process reflecting the two factors influencing it: capital and welfare. The first acts towards more and more homogenization whereas the second towards more and more differentiation. The problem of postmodern civilization and its destiny will depend on its capability to lead the opposition to harmony and opposite poles to coincidence by preserving the differences and finally achieving coherence and order, even a new type of unity. My answer is based on the idea of co-existence and 'convergence', confirming Sang Lee and David Olson's 'convergence revolution' (2010).

Therefore, not only have I created a picture of an overly complex and varied shape of welfare theories based on a new reference framework, but also draw attention to the quest for welfare as a phenomenon bearing a multi-scalar manifestation, calling for a renovated debate. The first level of this research endeavour begins, as already mentioned, with an examination of a diversified theoretical debate, circumscribing Esping-Andersen's model of the 'Three Worlds'.

CHAPTER I

REVIEWING CONCEPTS AND METHODS IN THE WELFARE TYPOLOGY BUSINESS

On 'Welfare Capitalism'

ESPING-ANDERSEN'S PERSPECTIVE ON WELFARE CAPITALISM FACILITATES the economic approach to the 'welfare-state complex' (1990, p. 2), making a distinction between narrow and broad views of the welfare state (1990, p. 2). According to Esping-Anderson, the broad approach includes not only 'income transfers and social services', but foremost all the other elements that determine the 'macroeconomic stirring' and facilitate the concept of the welfare-state within the dynamic of the capitalist system (Ibid).

Esping-Anderson's definition of a 'regime' is the 'complex of legal and organizational features" which are "systematically interwoven" between a state and its economy' (Ibid).

In addition, Esping-Andersen defines 'welfare state regimes' as:

> [Denoting] the institutional arrangements, rules and understandings that guide and shape concurrent social policy decisions, expenditure developments, problem definitions, and even the respond-and-demand structure of citizens and welfare consumers. The existence of policy regimes reflects the circumstance that short-term policies,

reforms, debates, and decision-making take place within frameworks of historical institutionalization that differ qualitatively between countries (Ibid, p. 80).

Based on this differentiation, the author concludes that the entire variety of welfare state situations can be classified into three distinct worlds of welfare capitalism.

Concerned with variations of welfare regimes across countries, Esping-Andersen advanced his regime-type classifications, forming a new basis for welfare capitalism. His initial regime typology was based on 18 OECD (Organisation for Economic Co-operation and Development) countries, grouping them based on the *index of de-commodification* and *welfare-state stratification*.

As we survey international variations in social rights and welfare-state stratification, we will find qualitatively different arrangements between state, market, and the family. The welfare-state variations we find are therefore not linearly distributed, but clustered by regime types. (Ibid, p. 26)

De-commodification is how the arrangement between state, market and the family results in the family having an advantage over the market. The weight of this relative advantage is a measure of the de-commodification index used as a criteria for different welfare regimes. The comparative literature on welfare regimes is also split into varieties of decommodification potential.

Contrasting 'worlds' of de-commodification

ESPING-ANDERSEN'S ARGUMENT IN FAVOUR OF DE-COMMODIFICATION was essentialized by Polanyi (1944), through what he considered what fundamentally determined de-commodification:

> The major tragedy attendant on the Industrial Revolution was brought about not by the callousness and greed of profit-seeking capitalists— though there was inhumanity enough in the record—but by the social devastation of an uncontrolled system, the market economy. Men failed to

realize what the cohesion of society meant. (Polanyi, K., 1944, p. x)

Esping-Anderson elaborated further, describing de-commodification as a 'process with multiple roots':

> It is, as Polanyi argued, necessary for system survival. It is also a precondition for a tolerable level of individual welfare and security. Finally, without de-commodification, workers are incapable of collective action [...] (Esping-Anderson, 1990, p. 37)

Powell, M. (2015) noticed the various degrees of comprehending the concept of de-commodification. Esping-Andersen's (1990) work 'on de-commodification [...] draws on Marshall (1963)' although:

> There appear to be three main differences between de-commodification and Marshallian citizenship. First, [...] writers such as Marshall and Crosland did not consider that all services should be free. Second, de-commodification assumes no relationship between market position and welfare [...] Third, with particular reference to cash benefits, de-commodification, is clear that benefits are inviolable and pitched at replacement wage levels. (Powell, M., 2002, p. 236)

Powell also noted that Esping-Andersen 'writes that the *minimal* definition of de-commodification entails that "citizens can freely, and without potential loss of job, income, or general welfare, opt out of work when they themselves consider it necessary"' (Esping-Andersen, G., 1990, p. 23, cited in Powell, M., 2015, p. 249).

Esping-Andersen (1990) used the multi-dimensional perspective on the 'de-commodifying potential' of welfare policies to compare his selected 18 OECD nations. He presented:

> Combined scores of de-commodification for the three most important social-welfare programs: pensions, sickness, and unemployment cash-benefits. [...] The overall de-commodification scores are weighted by the percent of the relevant population covered by the social security program. (Esping-Andersen, 1990, p. 49)

In addition, the overall index of de-commodification was determined by analysing the weighted sum of the three constituents of the index (i.e. pensions, sickness, and unemployment cash-benefits).

Many commentators refer to Esping-Andersen's classification as an 'ideal mode of categorisation', but it still receives criticisms regarding the validity of his methodological construct. C. Bambra revisited some of Esping-Andersen's methodological assumptions, focusing on the construct of his now famous de-commodification index:

> [The] indexes may not in fact be analyzing decommodification but rather programme coverage rates and this has implications for how the typology is interpreted. (Bambra, C., 2006, p. 12)

Moreover, Kasza (2002) spotted welfare variations 'across different areas of social provision' (Bambra, C., 2005, p. 32), making 'the concept of welfare regimes [...] not a workable basis for research' (Kasza, 2002, p. 283). The welfare regime is based on 'a set of principles or values that establishes a coherence in each country's welfare package' (Kasza, 2002, p. 272, apud Bambra, C., 2005, p. 31). Each country's welfare state is a 'world' in itself, dependent on:

> Diverse histories of different policy areas within a country's welfare framework; the variation of policy actors across different fields; differences in the policy making process; and the influence on policy of external/foreign welfare models [...] (Bambra, C., 2005, p. 31)

Nevertheless, clustering variations in the 'index of de-commodification' became a central theme in Esping-Andersen's work (1990). He started his journey of empirical construction by firstly considering the dimension of decommodification. The new method based on scoring the indices of de-commodification reveals a new broader conceptual meaning of the 'welfare regime'. De-commodification is the process through which the 'wage earners' escape market dependence. Consequently, the concept of de-commodification has become a 'central characteristic of the welfare state' (Huo, J. et al., 2008).

The conceptual clarification of 'welfare regime' needs further developments, as de-commodification alone provides a rather mixed perspective in the comparative analysis of welfare regimes. Although 'Esping- Andersen's ideal-types of welfare state regimes are holistic' (Arts, W., Gelissen, J., 2002, p. 139), further evidence is needed to incorporate characteristics of the realities, such as stratification, welfare mix as well as other conceptual and analytical frameworks, e.g. historical institutionalism (Thelen, K., 1999; Steinmo, S., 2008; Skocpol, T., 1995; Inglot, T., 2008) and critical reviews (cf. Ferragina E., Seeleib-Kaiser M., 2011).

Identifying 'salient dimensions' of stratifications and public-private mix

ESPING-ANDERSEN DISCOVERED 'DIFFERENT LOGICS OF SOCIAL stratification embedded in "welfare-state construction"' (1990, p. 77). As already noted, one major contribution of his three-worlds typology rests, on the dimensional variety of welfare regimes.

Therefore, the dimensions of de-commodification and stratification become embedded into the logic of a typological approach, such as the one developed by Esping-Andersen (1990). It opens up a new perspective in comparative welfare state research, as new meanings are added in the process of conceptual transformation (cf. Beckert, J., 2007). In light of this, scholars continued to tackle neglected dimensions in the comparative welfare state developments. For instance, Powell, M. and Barrientos, A. (2004) revealed two *neglected areas* in Esping-Andersen's regime typology: the 'identification of welfare regimes' and 'the role of the welfare mix' (Powell, M., Barrientos, A., 2011, p. 84).

Esping-Andersen built bridges between three 'salient dimensions' of welfare regimes: *de-commodification, stratification* and *public-private mix*. This is similar to 'bridging the worlds of work and welfare' (Ibid) in the case of active labour market policies. The worlds of welfare regimes are not only clustered in regime-types, but also 'embedded in welfare-state construction' (Esping-Andersen, 1990, p. 77) The concept of 'embeddedness' makes the syntagma of *"bridging the worlds of welfare"* more comprehensible.

Embeddedness leads to dimensional varieties based on linking various conceptual dimensions and variables to their analytical representation. For instance, the de-commodification potential, as a conceptual dimension, is placed in a new analytical representation designated by the world of welfare regimes. Other dimensional varieties are the worlds of stratification and welfare and 'the worlds of work and welfare' (Powell, M., Barrientos, A., 2011, p. 84). Each 'salient' dimensional variety of welfare regime is embedded in its corresponding world. For instance, the 'degree of universalism' is embedded in the world of social-democratic regime. Indeed, context matters in arriving at a representation of welfare realities.

'Context matters': contextual designations

THE ISSUE OF CONTEXTUAL DESIGNATIONS IS STILL UNSETTLED IN THE regime literature, with key concepts sometimes used interchangeably. 'Welfare-state regime' is the 'organizing concept' of Esping-Andersen's *Three Worlds of Welfare Capitalism* (1990). This triadic world of welfare capitalism has the 'welfare regime' as its main variation. In the same way, Bambra (2007) delineates the Conservative regime as 'Conservative welfare state regime'. Thus, the usability of key concepts is somehow inter-changeable as, for instance, the concept of 'welfare regime' is used instead of 'welfare state regime' when delineating a particular world. The conceptual designation as part of the context needs further clarification in the 'welfare modelling business'. Abrahamson's study 'concludes that welfare typologizing must take into account the kinds of programmes analysed: context matters' but Esping-Andersen merely touched upon several explanatory variables, including the 'welfare ideology', 'historical development', 'simple accounts of expenditure level or geographical position' and 'institutional features' (Abrahamson, 1999, p. 412). The 'context dependency' needs a better positioning strategy within the 'welfare modelling business' as, for instance, the 'historical developments' played a significant role in the emergence of welfare regimes in parts of the world such as regimes from Central and Eastern Europe. Once more, such a positioning strategy needs an overarching approach to welfare regimes that should take into account not only the context, but also the conceptual clarification as well as the methods and theoretical perspectives that would add up to the grounded construction of types and typologies of welfare regimes.

In conclusion, we underline again that, although 'the three worlds of welfare capitalism' opened up the debate on classifying the worlds of welfare regimes, a question remains: 'should we consider welfare capitalism to come in two, three, four or more models?' (Abrahamson, 1999). Such a question leads us to the problem of 'case selection' in comparative studies.

Worlds – number and composition

THE PROBLEMS OF CASE SELECTION GAINED TRACTION IN THE literature on comparative studies (cf. Ki-tae Kim, 2015). Some commentators argued that there is 'a fourth "Southern" world of welfare emerges into which Italy can also be placed' (Bonoli J., Castles F, Mitchell D., Ferrera, M, Leibfreid S. apud Bambra, C. 2007). A fifth world is the 'Confucian welfare state regime' (Aspalter C., Croissant A., Walker A, Wong C., apud Bambra, 2007). Martin Powell and Ki-tae Kim (2014) suggested that exporting Esping-Andersen's typology to other parts of the world, needs 'a change in strategy (concepts and measures)', so that we are requested to shed a light on the problems of the non-canonical 'welfare worlds', that is, on the worlds which appears to be undisciplinable when referred to the so called 'general models' (universalistic typologies).

The non-canonical 'welfare worlds'

ONE MAJOR ISSUE STILL RAISES FURTHER CLARIFICATIONS: ARE THE NEW emergent welfare states from the less developed 'worlds' 'in the process of emulating the Western model, or are they following qualitatively new trajectories?' (Esping-Andersen, 1996, p. 20).

Esping-Andersen's 'worlds' of welfare are based on his initial selection of 18 OECD nations (1990) - adding Spain and Portugal to his list in 1999.

Finally, he spotted three additional 'trajectories' (Esping-Andersen, 1994). The first comprised of countries from South America (Argentina, Chile) and East-Central Europe, which 'broadly' matched the characteristics of a liberal regime. A second group (Brazil and Costa Rica) was of nations that exhibited neo-liberal traits. His third 'trajectory', the East Asian group, indicated a mix of unique and hybrid Western 'arrangements', which still endorsed the existing classification. Ki-tae Kim suggested that a 'wider coverage of nations and indicators' (2015, p. 311) was needed alongside promoting a multilateral strategy. In other words, it is time for the welfare modelling business 'to go "global"', and freeing the business from 'its unilateral Swedocentrism, Eurocentrism or ethnocentrism' has become an imperative (Takegawa, 2009; Walker and Wong, 2013). 'Exporting [...] West-rooted concepts to "other worlds"' should be combined with '"importing" concepts or variables from "other worlds"' (Ki-tae Kim, 2015, p. 316).

There needs to be further exploration of the neglected 'worlds' of welfare regimes, leading to new conceptual approaches and clarification of alternatives paths. As such, the worlds of welfare state regimes became representational phenomena pertaining to a modelling approach. Frigg, R. and Hartmann, S. (2012) considered that the scientific model is 'an umbrella term covering all relatively stable and general features of the world that are interesting from a scientific point of view.' The next section is focused on clarifying the dynamic relationship between different typological constructs in the remarkable literature on welfare regimes rooted in Esping-Andersen's 'three worlds of welfare capitalism'.

A contributory introduction to the study of 'welfare modelling phenomena'

ESPING-ANDERSEN'S THEORETICAL AND EMPIRICAL INCURSION IN the 'worlds of welfare capitalism' opens up the debate on systematically reviewing the 'worlds' of welfare regimes. Deepening Esping-Andersen's analysis, Taylor-Gooby (1996, p. 199) argues that the notion of *welfare capitalism* might be invoked as a 'point of departure [on which] we can draw the following definition of a regime':

> A regime is understood as a particular constellation of
> social, political and economic arrangements which tend to
> nurture a particular welfare system, which in turn supports
> a particular pattern of stratification, and thus feeds back
> into its own stability. (Ibid)

Nevertheless, Taylor-Gooby's definition of "regime" points to nurturing a 'particular welfare system' (Ibid). Can we find welfare without capitalism? (Powell, M., 2015)

Thus, comprehension of the welfare regimes requires us to make a distinction between different regimes via comparative analysis. via comparative analysis. Comparing welfare realities has gained momentum since the seminal contributions of Esping-Andersen (1990). National welfare systems differ in clusters of nations: there are countries belonging to Nordic Social-Democratic regimes called the 'Nordic model',[1] the conservative welfare regimes known as Continental or European regimes[2] and Liberal regimes.[3] Using Esping-Andersen's 'three ideal-type categories' (Ebbinghaus, B., 2012), these three welfare regime types have become the pivotal conceptual framework in the comparative analysis of social policy in the last three decades.

Early exponents of 'welfare state typologizing'

RICHARD TITMUSS, ONE OF THE EARLY EXPONENTS OF VARIOUS perspectives on welfare regimes, made the 'distinction between "three contrasting models" or functions of social policy institutionalist, handmaiden and residual models' (Titmuss, 1974, p. 30). Powell and Barrientos examined the similarities and distinctions between Titmuss' classification and Esping-Andersen's typology in a structured way,

---

1   Also called 'Nordic capitalism' (Eklund, K. et al., 2011) or Nordic social democracy (Bratberg, Ø et al., 2013). Examples include Denmark, Finland, Norway, Iceland, Sweden and the Netherlands.

2   Also called the 'Bismarckian' model. Examples include Germany, Austria, Italy, France, Belgium and Spain.

3   Examples include the United Kingdom, the United States, Canada, New Zealand and Australia.

suggesting several key elements in comparing the two typologies:

> First, Titmuss' primary focus was on the provision of services (see above). Second, he was perhaps above all concerned with values and the 'ends' of social policy (Titmuss 1974, p. 32). [...] Wildeboer Schut et al (2001, p. 149) claim that Titmuss model focuses on the traditional objectives of the welfare state: protection against loss in income, combating poverty and limiting social inequality. (Powell, M., Barrientos, A., 2011, p. 9)

Peter Flora (1986) noted that 'most typologies start with the distinction between three "models of social policy" due to Titmuss (1974)':

> (A)   residual welfare model in which social welfare institutions come into play only if the private market and the family as the "natural" channels for the fulfilment of social needs break down;

> (B)   industrial achievement-performance model in which social welfare institutions are adjuncts of the economy, and social needs are met on the basis of merit, work performance and productivity;

> (C)   institutional redistributive model in which social welfare institutions are an integral part of society, providing universalist services outside the market on the principle of need. (Flora, P. 1986, p. xxi)

We shall note the similarities between Titmuss' typology and the 'Three Worlds', although Esping-Andersen's welfare regimes are shaped by political forces:

> As we do not find the association between regimes and political parties that straightforward we prefer the labels: *Residual, universal* and *corporatist* welfare model. (Andersen, J. G., 2012, p. 6)

Powell and Barrientos, on their turn, argued that the 'origins of welfare modelling are far from clear' (2011, p. 5). 'The residual welfare model' (Titmuss, R., 1974, p. 30) is similar to Esping-Andersen's liberal welfare regime. The rise of the 'residual welfare model' (as Titmuss denoted it) induced by the breakdown of the 'natural channels' (Flora, P., 1986) (private markets and family) is similar to Esping-Andersen's liberal regime, where only 'people who are unable to help themselves' (Lodemel, I., 1989, p. 11) are entitled to social benefits. Therefore, we can assert that Titmuss' model is quite similar to a liberal model of welfare state, where such needs are fulfilled through the redistribution of 'benefits [that] cater mainly to a clientele of low-income, usually working class, state dependents' (Esping-Andersen, G., 1990, p. 26, cited in Pierson, C., Castles, F. G., 2006, p. 167). 'The industrial achievement-performance model' (Titmuss, R., 1974, p. 31), on its turn, incorporates a strong commitment to meritocracy, work performance and productivity as a condition for granting social benefits to those in need. Similarly, the legacy of conservative welfare regime is based on granting social rights:

> [That are] conditional upon morals, loyalties, or convention, also evident in the statist tradition, historically perhaps best exemplified in the regimes of Germany under Bismarck, and von Taaffe's Austria. (Esping-Andersen, G., 1990, p. 40)

The readiness of conservatism to redistribute social welfare based on meritocracy, morality or convention is similar to Titmuss' main assumptions on the existence of 'the industrial achievement-performance model' (1974, p. 31). 'The institutional redistributive model' (Ibid) advocates a universalistic approach to the redistribution of social welfare in society. The social benefits are granted to all in need based on the 'principles of universalism' (Pierson, C; Castles, F.G., 2006, p. 168) stemming from the 'Beveridge principle of universal rights of citizenship, regardless of degree of need or extent of work performance' (Esping-Andersen, G., 1990, p. 48).

Arts, W. and Gelissen, J. (2002) systematically reviewed the traditional literature on comparative social policy, arguing that there are *two main analytical dimensions* for the empirical and theoretical foundation of Esping- Andersen's typology:

> *(A)   Theoretically,* the work of Marshall (1950; 1963; 1965; 1981) and Titmuss (1958; 1974) laid the foundations for Esping-Andersen's typology (Boje, 1996, p. 19).

(B)   Empirically, he could profit from the comparative research by, among others, Wilensky (1975), Flora and Heidenheimer (1981), Mommsen (1981) and Flora (1983; 1986). (Arts, W.; Gelissen, J., 2002, p. 138)

Thus, the studies of Marshall and Titmuss lay the groundwork for a critical analysis of Esping-Andersen's classifications. Such various accounts lead to different theoretical perspectives which often collide, therefore leading to such contrasting 'worlds'. We are confronted not only with 'worlds' of welfare regimes but with 'worlds' of theoretical and empirical perspectives. Therefore, Esping-Andersen's typology preserves its epistemological role in welfare regimes developments, and we shall refer to it based on this conclusion.

Empirical critique. The pivotal issue of welfare state origins

MOST CRITIQUES OF ESPING-ANDERSEN'S TYPOLOGY ARE EMPIRICAL (Powell, M; Barrientos, A. 2011, p. 11), mediating the roadmap to a renovated approach on the 'theoretical substance of welfare states' (Esping-Andersen, G., 1990, p. 19, apud Powell, M; Barrientos, A. 2011, p. 11). The methodology and 'art of typifying the welfare state regimes' is closely linked to welfare state origins, being that it appears dependent not only on economic but on cultural and historical (and therefore, empirical) grounds.

Therefore, a brief examination of empirical critics of Esping-Andersen's typology proves to be much more than merely an answer to an exigency. As a matter of fact, looking for an answer to such a question leads us to the determinant factors of welfare state origin. Were such factors economically, cultural or politically driven? Esping-Andersen's typology received 'wide critical acclaim and constructive criticism, but also some negative criticism' (Arts, W.; Gelissen, J., 2002, p. 138). Arts, W. and Gelissen, J. arrived at three 'pivotal questions' after reviewing 'the state of the art of typifying welfare states at the turn of the millennium'(Ibid):

How and why has the welfare state developed?

How and why do national welfare systems differ from one another – or are they similar to each other?

Do welfare states cluster into different regime types and, if so, how[,] why and when? (Ibid)

Peter Flora argues that:

> The origins of the Western European welfare states reach back to the nineteenth century, some of their present institutional features predating the First World War. Their present format, however, is mainly a product of the "golden age of the welfare state" from the early 1960s to the mid-1970s, when the world-wide economic crisis put an end to the historically unprecedented expansion. (Flora, P, 1986, p. XII)

A. Briggs (1961) claims that the concept of 'welfare state' is of 'recent origin', being firstly 'used to describe Labour Britain after 1945'. (Briggs, A., 1961) Scholars, politicians and journalists started to use the concept of 'welfare state' in relation to a variety of social problems 'at diverse stages of development' (Ibid) ever since. Although there has been a significant attempt towards explaining the welfare state through a historical lens, there has nevertheless been a strong incentive towards considering political factors as a strong determinant of welfare state development, such as how Esping-Andersen (1990) pointed towards a political determination. Let's examine the issue on this distinct facet.

Welfare state as a power resource: activating 'class mobilization thesis'

THE NOVELTY OF ESPING-ANDERSEN' SEMINAL STUDY ON THE "THREE Worlds" is that it explains the variations of the welfare state, using the *'power resource approach'* (Aidukaite, 2009), with 'the welfare state itself being regarded as a power resource' (Esping-Andersen, 1990, p. 16). Esping-Andersen activated the 'class mobilization thesis', emphasizing that the 'welfare state itself is a power resource' (Ibid), a pivotal idea for his thesis' applicability. The class-mobilization theory has some 'valid objections', the most fundamental concerning the 'model's linear view of power' (Ibid, p. 17). The political power is not linearly distributed: 'a more numerical increase in votes, unionization or seats' will not necessarily 'translate into more welfare-statism'. (Ibid, p. 17) Is Esping-Andersen hinting towards a major shift in the welfare theory development?

Olsen, G. and Connor, J. argue that:

> The emphasis power resources theory placed on comparative and quantitative studies of the relationship between social policy and labour mobilization enabled it to provide a more satisfying explanation for wide variations in the development and outcome of welfare states across the industrialized nations than of many other accounts. (1998, p. 3)

Social class as a political agent has the power to configure and re-configure the welfare state although social class *per se*, cannot infuse the change at societal level in terms of social welfare redistribution. Social class needs political mobilization to translate into its manifest way, and welfare statism represents the practices of a welfare state. The 'class-coalitional approach' indeed has 'additional virtues', but it foremost has the power and the necessary determination to move society towards its socially desirable outcome (Esping-Andersen, G., 1990, p. 18).

The patterns of political activity are shaped by welfare states but, at the same time, such patterns have the power to shape the different configurations of the welfare state.

The main argument of the power resource approach is that the impact of the ruling parties is significant regarding social policy development. (Aidukaite, J., 2009, p. 27)

Aidukaite believes that the level of welfare state development depends on the 'impact of ruling political parties on social policy reform [[...]]' (Aidukaite, J., 2009, p. 27) Esping-Andersen's theoretical underpinnings regarding the 'power resource approach' to 'social policy development' point towards the impact of the 'class-coalitional approach' on the 'welfare statism'. The configuration of the class-coalitional approach provides a new perspective on the determining factors of welfare statism:

> We have to think in terms of social relations not just social categories. Whereas structural functionalist explanations

identify convergent welfare-state outcomes, and class mobilization paradigms see large, but linearly distributed, differences, an interactive model such as the coalition approach directs attention to distinct welfare-state regimes. (Esping-Andersen, G., 1990, p. 18)

Functionalism explains the welfare state 'as a convenience to capitalism, a "shock absorber", as John Saville has called it' (Wedderburn, D., 1965, p. 137). Functionalist explanations converge towards the same intended outcome which is 'the collective recognition of certain socially determined needs' (Ibid: 138). The socio-political relations built upon coalitions as the new agents of welfare state offer a new meaning and a new path towards clarifying the factors impacting the dynamic of welfare state.

A 'class-coalitional approach' becomes central to Esping-Andersen's theoretical perspective on welfare regimes, explaining how welfare states were shaped by 'conditions for power mobilization' (Esping-Andersen, G., 1990, p. 18). The 'power resource approach' (Aidukaite, J., 2009) significantly contributed to the paradigmatic development of welfare state theories. 'Structural-functionalist explanations, [...][...] class mobilization paradigms [and] the coalition approach' (Esping-Andersen, G., 1990, p. 18) contributed towards what Kutash E. invoked as the 'fecundity of a paradigmatic formula [that] can predict and explain phenomena' (Kutash, E., 2011, p. 84) not only in the 'physical world' but, also, in the 'social reality' (Smith, B., 2003). The 'coalition approach' provides the 'interactive model' within such a 'paradigmatic formula' which 'directs attention to distinct welfare states regimes' (Esping-Andersen, G., 1990, p. 18).

The linear approach to his activated 'class mobilization thesis' became debatable as 'in very few cases has the traditional working class been numerically a majority' (Esping-Andersen, G., 1990, p. 17). The 'welfare-state variations [...] are not linearly distributed, but clustered by regime-types.' (Pierson, C., Castles, F. G. 2006, p. 167):

> Esping-Andersen (1990, p. 3, 26, 32) boldly suggests that when we focus on the principles embedded in welfare states, variations are not linearly distributed around a common denominator. They are clustered around three

highly diverse regime-types, each organized according to
its own discrete logic of organization, stratification, and
societal integration. (Arts, W; Gelissen, J., 2002, p. 139)

As such, Esping-Andersen makes the case for grouping welfare regimes
into distinct clusters. His politically-driven 'interactive model' provides
the rationale for clustering 'welfare-state variations' into 'regime-types'.
Moreover, 'a theory of welfare state developments must clearly reconsider
its causal assumptions': 'the nature of (especially working-) class
mobilization; class-political coalition structures; and the historical legacy
of regime institutionalization' (Olsen, G. and Connor, J., 1998, p. 144).
There is no one single causal explanation for clustering welfare regimes
(Ibid). Esping-Andersen (1990) arrived at his now famous three 'worlds' of
welfare regimes based on the power resource theory:

> The more political resources the working class can muster,
> such as a strong and united union movement providing
> electoral support to Labour or Social Democratic parties,
> the more extensive, comprehensive, universal, and
> generous the welfare state will become (Esping-Andersen,
> 1990) (Rothstein, B. et al, 2012, p. 3)

Nevertheless, the power resource theory regards political institutions
as 'simple arenas for conflict among social classes or as useful political
tools for the parties involved in this struggle' (Rothstein, B. et al, 2012, p.
2). Deepening the problematic of "causal assumptions" in welfare theory
developments reveals a marginalization of historical and institutional
developments. The 'quality of government' plays a significant role in
shaping welfare state configurations. There is still much to be done
when considering the conceptual and theoretical aspects of welfare state
developments.

Esping-Andersen's typology triggered the debate surrounding the
problems of welfare states configuration. Abrahamson noticed the
momentous change in the theories and methodological directions infused
by Esping Andersen' seminal study:

> Different typologies with different degrees of differentiation
> are discussed: should we consider welfare capitalism to

come in two, three, four or more models? (Abrahamson, 1999)

Scholars have embarked on a quest to find answers to such questions. A special point refers to the neglect of CEE nations in welfare modelling business and Esping-Andersen (EA) model is, indeed, too 'Nordic' centred. The question is:

> Can EA approach/ criteria/ indicators be extended to nations with very different histories, and social and political structures? Can CEE be included as another 'world' – e.g. the 4ᵗʰ or 5ᵗʰ - beyond EA's 3 worlds? Are CEE nations so different that can't be examined within EA Nordic-centred account? (Powell, M., 2015)

The large theoretical debate on 'welfare capitalism' went far beyond the boundaries of Western capitalism

WELFARE REGIMES IN THE CEE WENT, ESPECIALLY AFTER 1989, THROUGH a transformational process pertaining to high volatility realities, where periods of circumstantial prosperity alternated with moments of retrenchment recurrently over decades of historical evolutions.

The historical conditionality in the CEE has contributed to the emergence of a new typological perspective on welfare regimes. The dynamic of the welfare state permeates a meta or paradigmatic welfare regime consisting of that framing perspective helping us to find out the significant connections between different models, types and theories of the welfare regimes. As the theories of welfare 'operate above the more focused debates on particular problems or concepts [...] they are sometimes referred to as metanarratives' (Alcock, P, Powell, M., 2011, p. 4). The 'paradigmatic regimes' allows for expanding the boundaries of the debate on the 're-specification of the welfare state' (Esping-Andersen, 1990) induced by its spatial and temporal variation.

Here are some examples of references to the paradigmatic regimes: 'The "Chameleon" Korean Welfare Regime' (Powell and Ki-tae Kim, 2014); 'Three Worlds of Welfare Capitalism' (Esping-Andersen, 1990);

Post-communist 'Emergency' welfare states (Inglot, 2008); CEE's welfare regimes configured by the residual role of the culturally sub- alternate political elite's style of life.

> Theories of welfare is therefore the term used to refer to
> the more sophisticated ideological frameworks developed
> by academics and aiming to provide an overall explanation
> of how social policy could, and should, be understood.
> (Alcock, P., Powell, M., 2011, p. 1)

The comparative literature on welfare states has confirmed that the debate is rather slanted towards exploring the main ideas infused by seminal studies (cf. Esping-Andersen, 1990) instead of providing explanatory frameworks.

Esping-Andersen's three worlds' typology has become one of the principal heuristics for examining modern welfare states. (Powell and Barrientos, 2015). Could Esping-Andersen's 'three worlds typology' be considered a 'paradigmatic regime'?

> It relates to the dilemma of whether welfare regimes are
> primarily variable–oriented latent ideal type configurations,
> or whether they are primarily case-oriented country
> configurations. (Ibid, p. 244)

There is still the third perspective, i.e. the paradigmatic typology that is not an 'ideal type' (Weber, M., 1922).[4] The paradigmatic typology

---

4   A brief examination of the concept of ideal type seems to be instrumental to the next exertion. I will blank out a comment on Max Weber's concept: 'In his effort to escape from the individualizing and particularizing approach of German Geisteswissenschaft and historicism, Weber developed a key conceptual tool, the notion of the ideal type. It will be recalled that Weber argued that no scientific system is ever capable of reproducing all concrete reality, nor can any conceptual apparatus ever do full justice to the infinite diversity of particular phenomena. All science involves selection as well as abstraction. Yet the social scientist can easily be caught in a dilemma when he chooses his conceptual apparatus. When his concepts are very general--as when he attempts to explain capitalism or Protestantism by subsuming them under the general concepts of economics or religion--he is likely to leave out what is most distinctive to them. When, on the other hand, he uses the traditional conceptualizations of the historian and particularizes the phenomenon under discussion, he allows no room for comparison with related phenomena. The notion of the ideal type was meant to provide escape from this dilemma.' From Coser, 1977, p. 223-224.) (Source: http://msumainsocioanthro.blogspot.com/ [26.07.2019])

of welfare regimes describes a pattern of institutional and political arrangements generated over a long period of time, stretching back over decades of social, economic and political transformations. This is certainly the case with welfare regimes from the CEE (See Inglot, T., 2008). We need to differentiate between the causal factors (pivotal factor) and conditional factors of a welfare regime. Wilensky makes such a distinction between industrialism as a root cause of welfare state and some special conditions which operate as over-determinations on the process:

> [Economic] level is the root cause of welfare state development, but its effects are felt chiefly through the demographic changes of the past century and the momentum of the programs themselves, once. established. (Wilensky, H., 1975, p. 47)

Welfare state effort was correlated with affluence, suggesting that 'strong economies produce strong welfare states.' (Pierson, 1996, pp. 143-179).

> Without doubt, the economy and the welfare state are intertwined. In a study of welfare state economic relations, Esping-Andersen (1994) concludes that the welfare state is not something opposed to or, in some way, related to the economy. Instead, it is an integral element of the organic linkage of production, reproduction, and consumption, none of which can survive without the others. (Aidukaite, 2009, p. 30)

This organic linkage composes the framework of what will finally induce the re-specification process of the welfare regimes from one regional worlds to another.

Convergence-divergence paradigm on the welfare state developments in the CEE countries

THERE ARE SOME CONVERGING PHENOMENA THAT CAUSED THE PROCESS of 're- specification of the welfare state':

    a) Multiple tensions emerged within the 'Europeanization' process (the extension of the Western type of 'institutional capitalism', that is, the inflowing in Eastern societies of the capitalist forms of organizing collective life; such a top-down penetration of capitalism used to be improperly called 'Europeanization').

b) Convergence versus polarization.

c) Local versus European social problems.

d) The European versus national architecture of welfare state.

e) The market forces versus politics and societal pressures.

All of these operate as converging pressure on a local context determining the phenomenon of the welfare regimes' re-specification within such a context. An example for such converging social pressures is the 'negative salary', that is, the amount of un-cashed salaries due to austerity measures in a country, such as the well-known effects of austerity measures in Greece due to the government-debt crisis.[5] Another type of social pressure is referring to the dangerous degradation of social security because of the low expenses in the field of social services etc. We may speak therefore about a *divergence of welfare state developments in the CEE countries as compared to Western types.* Draxler, J. and Olaf Van Vliet (2010) conclude that there is no 'convergence from the East'. The European Social Model becomes a field of a dystopia rather than an affordable model for all:

> Our analysis based on expenditure data, then, confirms that the post-communist EU member states tend to show certain resilience to convergence with a generalized ESM. They spend less on social policy. (Draxler, Van Vliet, op. cit., p. 232)

Briggs (1945) points out that we need a 'minimum standard' from where to start while carrying out comparative welfare state research, advancing the concept of 'social service state' (Briggs, cited in Alcock & Powell, 2011).

---

5   Up to 64,000 Greeks worked without pay and some even had to pay for having a job. More on this issue: https://www.theatlantic.com/international/archive/2012/02/some-greeks-might-have-pay-their-jobs/331427/ (accessed 09.08.2020)

On this aspect, we may notice a new sort of European polarization between the West where the 'fiscal and occupational welfare tend to be regressive' (cf. Powell and Alcock, 2011, p. 3), favouring so the middle class, and the East, where the fiscal and occupational welfare is progressive and public welfare is regressive.[6] No matter how severe polarization and inequality could be when comparing West and East, North and South, the challenge remains equally demanding as to the tension between convergence and divergence of welfare realities. A unification of the diversity is required to make the issue comprehensible through its own converging, diverging distribution and dynamic.

'Path dependency' of welfare state evolution

THE SECOND CHALLENGE FOR THOSE WHO LOOK FOR A UNIFIED perspective towards a re-specification of welfare state results from the path dependency of welfare state evolution. Esping-Andersen (1990) points out that 'politics and political institutions play the leading role' in re-shaping the worlds of 'welfare capitalism'. Assuming the idea of a much wider literature on welfare situations, Myles, J. and Quadagno, J. speak about two phases in the evolution of welfare state: a first one characterised by a 'slow growth of the social programs associated with Bismarck's Germany in the 1880s' and a phase characterised by 'the post-war boom in welfare state expansion (the period of high industrialism) that came to maturity (and to an end) in the mid-1970s':

> From the mid-1970s to the early 1990s welfare state research concentrated on the long slow growth of the social programs associated with Bismarck's Germany in the 1880s to the post-war boom in welfare state expansion (the period of high industrialism) that came to maturity (and to an end) in the mid-1970s. The puzzle to be solved was less about why welfare states developed than with why they had developed in such different ways and apparently reached their apogee at such strikingly different levels of spending.

---

6   On the occupational welfare, a concept coined by Titmuss, 1956, see Johnson, Norman (1987). The Welfare State in Transition: The Theory and Practice of Welfare Pluralism. Univ of Massachusetts Press. p. 137

> This body of scholarship can usefully be bracketed
> by two highly influential works: Harold Wilensky's
> (1975) *The Welfare State and Equality*, emphasizing the
> determining role of impersonal economic forces, and
> Esping-Andersen's (1990) *The Three Worlds of Welfare
> Capitalism*, where politics and political institutions play
> the leading role." (Miles, J. & Quadagno, J., 2002)

Therefore, although high industrialism is an axial factor of the post-war boom of welfare states throughout the world, it cannot explain by itself the real landscape of such a boom as long as the diversity remains un-explained. The diversity has to be ascribed to that complementary factor called 'dependency on the path'. The effect of this peculiar factor is another facet of the process of welfare regimes' re-specification and we have to take it into account in order to fully understand such a phenomenon. The idea of diverse predictors as to the expansion of the welfare state throughout the world appears as an added challenge for an epistemological examination of the welfare state expansion.

Diversity of predictors of welfare state evolution

AIDUKAITE UNDERLINES THAT ONE OF THE MAJOR CHALLENGES for scholars involved in comparative studies on welfare regimes is the determination of the predictors of both convergence and divergence of theories, types and models of welfare regimes.

> [In his comparative work,] which includes 22 affluent
> countries, Wilensky (2002) found that economic growth
> is no longer an independent predictor of welfare efforts.
> Affluence and ageing population (65 years old) account for
> most of the explanation. (Aidukaite, 2009, p. 29)

These factors contribute as additional predictors explaining the diversification and, therefore, re-specification of welfare states throughout different regions of the world.

> Without doubt, the economy and the welfare state are
> intertwined. In a study of welfare state economic relations,
> Esping-Andersen (1994) comes to the conclusion that the

welfare state ... is an integral element of the organic linkage
of production, reproduction, and consumption, none of
which can survive without the others. (J. Aidukaite 2009,
p. 30).

Another predictor is the ideological consensus (Blau, Joel, op. cit.) of the
post-WWII period, lasting till it disintegrates in the early 1970s. (See Blau,
Joel, op. cit., 1989, pp. 26-38), Its presence/absence might be invoked, as an
additional factor explaining the welfare expansion in time and space.

Social-policy deficit

WHILE MANY CENTRAL AND EASTERN EUROPEAN COUNTRIES BECAME
part of the European Union through the consecutive so-called 'waves',
the new EU member countries experienced different levels of welfare
state development. Therefore, some new EU members like the Czech
Republic, Poland and even Hungary have recorded more favourable
conditions of social and economic indicators comparative with other EU
countries from CEE. Comparing EU countries from CEE on the criterion
of the welfare state development will reveal a new perspective on welfare
regimes. What is the prevalent characteristic of the welfare regimes in
the selected CEE countries? Should we consider the residual role of the
political elite's style of life as being a significant characteristic of welfare
regimes differentiation in this part of the world? Instead of intervening
supportively in the redistribution, the political forces in Eastern Europe
appears to play a negative residual role. The governmental elites of the
region proceeded, with some exceptions, to privatizing state enterprises.
The 'Management Employee Buyouts' (MEBO), for instance, consisted in
the transfer of state-owned assets to employees.

[In Russia] privatization planners transferred 51%of
the stock in each company to its directors and workers.
Because the workers were not organized, the factory
directors gradually took over the entire amount. One class
of oligarchs, the factory directors, told the workers: 'Sell
me your stock or you'll be fired or shot' (Maltsev, Y. 2006,
p. 427)

The transition from communism to capitalism in the CEE led to the emergence of what Braguinsky Serguey (2007) called 'oligarchic capitalism', which has its roots in a 'politically-protected oligarchic property rights' (Serguey, B., 2007). Striking evidence of the residual role of political elites in CEE countries during the transition period was described by Mitchell A. Orenstein through the concept of 'social-policy deficit':

> The combination of 'immediate, severe crisis and the lack of significant economic-policy thinking on welfare-state transformation led to the adoption of a wide variety of "emergency measures" to combat the dramatic rise of poverty, unemployment, and other social crises.' (Claus Offe, 1993) Countries responded in a variety of ways to common policy pressures. Often these responses reflected the unique influence of small groups of expert policy makers in each country. Sometimes, ill-conceived 'emergency measures' created significant problems down the road. (Orenstein, 2008, p. 85)

These emergency measures act as a critical response to an "external shock" so that the social pressure of transitional period cumulated critical drawbacks along with the suddenly rise of poverty.

Social-policy deficit and 'shock policy'

THE SOCIAL-POLICY DEFICIT EMERGED AT THE BEGINNING OF THE so-called transition period for CEE countries. It is, probably, one of the most striking 'structural correlation' that induces differentiation of welfare regimes from CEE. Such 'emergency measures' as described by Orenstein (2008) could be explained through the well-known 'shock therapy' (Jeffrey Sachs), a term that gained significance during 'key junctures' where the ideology of neoliberalism 'took its leap forward – including Chile in 1973, China in 1989, Poland in 1989, Russia in 1993, and the Asian economic crisis in 1997 and 1998' (Reyes, O., 2007). The distortionary mechanisms in the CEE, partially explained through the consequences of the conditionality imposed by international financial institutions, were magnified by the set of macro-economic decisions that had a significant impact in the countries in transition. S. Polanec (2004) argues that price liberalization contributed to the output decline in transition countries from CEE. As Schumpeter (1908) argued, the *price policy* always acts as a redistributive method that deepens social and international inequality. Consequently, price liberalization contributed to the decline of purchasing power in these countries and therefore to a decline of welfare. Polanec, S. argued that:

> Liberalization of prices and trading relations after the collapse of the planning allocation mechanism leads to disorganization. [...] Under the assumption of either incomplete contracts or asymmetric information, the outcome of bargaining may be inefficient. In both cases buyers of inputs are unable to provide sellers an offer that would beat their outside option and thus output declines. (Polanec, S., 2003, p. 3)

We are facing a special type of distortionary mechanisms in the CEE, mechanisms opening a new perspective on its welfare regimes. The discussion turns to the investigation of representative cases of welfare states in the CEE. It is a perspective different from the one we used to know as 'ethnocentric western social research' (Jones, 1993). To understand the situation, we need to adjust the research by reviewing the literature on CEE welfare states.

CHAPTER II

CENTRAL AND EASTERN EUROPEAN WELFARE STATES

A still unsettled 'welfare modelling business'

THE COMPARATIVE LITERATURE ON WELFARE STATES IS MAINLY ROOTED in analytical constructs that 'deliberately, accentuate certain characteristics' (Smith, K. B., 2002) of welfare realities. Such analytical constructs led to typologies, the most famous one being Esping-Andersen's 'three worlds of welfare capitalism' (1990).

> Are typologies ideal-type constructs based on analytical concepts or are these only real-type categorizations that summarize cross-national variation of a selected group of countries? (Ebbinghaus, B., 2012, p. 1)

Answering this question demands further conceptual clarifications. First, 'the key characteristic of a typology is that its dimensions represent concepts rather than empirical cases' (Smith, K. B., 2002). Esping-Andersen's threefold classification (1990) is a typological construct as he arrived at the three 'worlds' of welfare capitalism by circumscribing his famous conceptual dimensions (i.e. decommodification and stratification). Such classification, on its turn, could have dimensions represented by empirical cases. For instance, some studies arrived at 'real types' (e.g. hybrid types) which are considered as empirical cases. One difference between typology and classification, is that arranging in classes based on conceptual dimensions produces categories (i.e. a generalizable representation of something), whereas classifying based on empirical evidence could produce empirical cases.

Our critical review revealed that studies of 'welfare worlds' are dominated by empirical cases, which are either hybrid, distinct or 'other' 'worlds'. The existence of typologies is essential to comparative literature on welfare states (cf. Ferragina E., Seeleib-Kaiser M., 2011), although the existing literature on welfare realities in the CEE points towards a still unsettled 'welfare modelling business' (Abrahamson, 1999).

Central and Eastern European 'typology business'

POWELL, M. AND BARRIENTOS, A. (2004) REVIEWED THE 'CONTRIBUTIONS to recent comparative social policy', considering the 'Three Worlds' as:

> [Leading] to a protracted debate on what Abrahamson (1999) identifies as 'the welfare modelling business' (Powell, M., Barrientos, A., 2004, p. 83)

The central argument points out the extensiveness of the 'welfare modelling business' 'in a manner that reflects diverse and highly significant cases beyond the Western lens that dominates the literature' (Powell, M., Kim, Ki-tae, 2014).

The meta-analysis of Ebbinghaus (2012), on its turn, points to the severe under-representation of CEE countries in comparative studies on welfare regimes. Moreover, while CEE nations have been neglected, the few studies debating the welfare realities in the CEE tend to use different concepts, variables and methods, and report different conclusions.

It is still not clear if the welfare states from the CEE can be categorised in terms of Esping-Andersen's regimes (liberal; conservative; social-democratic), as a separate 'world', or exhibiting overlapping features with Western-types (cf. the debate on the East Asian Welfare Model, Powell and Kim, 2014). One possible explanation for such a divergent manifestation of the 'worlds' of welfare in the CEE is that the analytical frameworks went beyond the boundaries of Western 'business typology' and the classifications confirm the existence of other than 'ideal types'.

Classificatory issues, aiming at 'welfare state regimes' (Esping-Andersen, 1999) as its core concept, took centre stage in academia since 1990 (cf. Abrahamson, 1999). Researchers discuss various approaches to welfare models, including general approaches, the Central and Eastern European Model (CEEWM), methodological (Barrientos, A., 2015), historical and institutionalist (Inglot, T., 2008). Moreover:

> [The] comparative welfare state research community has largely accepted the benefits of using ideal types and typologies as heuristic devices, as evidenced by the high number of references to Esping-Andersen's seminal work. (Ferragina, E., Seeleib-Kaiser, M., 2011, p. 585)

In terms of reflecting the CEE's 'typology business' in 'classic' texts, Esping-Andersen (1996) rejected the idea of a distinct Central and Eastern European Welfare Model (CEEWM) (see also, Sauer, T. et al., 2016), instead considering the European post-communist welfare states as converging towards one of his three-fold typology. Esping-Andersen opened the debate on the regime-type of the CEEWM, considering that there are 'no' '"new" trajectories [...] that deviate markedly from existing welfare states' (1996, p. 20). His assumption is based on his selection criteria (initially 18 OECD nations (1990), adding Spain and Portugal in 1999). Esping-Andersen (1996) suggested that the difference between his selected cases (Argentina, Chile, nations from the CEE, Brazil, Costa Rica and the 'Asian group') and the three Western-types 'were only of a transitional nature' (Fenger, M., 2007 apud Esping-Andersen, G., 1996).

Deacon suggested that a divergence between countries would be the most likely outcome of the transition process of East European welfare states, predicting that:

> [In] a few years' time we will be able to look back and characterize the social policy of these countries in terms that reflect Esping-Andersen's threefold typology, together with a new term that will have to be coined to describe the

unique post-communist conservative corporatism of parts of the one-time USSR, Romania, Bulgaria and parts of one-time Yugoslavia. (Deacon, 1993)

Scholars opted for a re-specification of CEE welfare regimes with only one exception found in one of Esping-Andersen's works (1994), that being East Central Europe, which 'follows a broadly liberal strategy'. Others considered CEE welfare states as being either 'incorporated' into an expanded 'threefold' typology (Fenger, 2007) or coined as 'post-communist conservative corporatism' (Deacon, 1993), 'emerging' regimes (Kuitto, K., 2016, Lendvai, N., 2009)l 'hybrid emerging' (Vanhuysse, P., 2016), 'transition regimes' (Žukowski, M., 2009), 'identifiable complexes' (Haggard, S., Kaufmann, R. R., 2008) or 'distinct/unified post-communist' welfare regimes (Aidukaite, J., 2011). Fenger (2007) included 47 countries (18 well-known Western states and 29 Central and Eastern European states as well as Central Asian countries) in a cluster analysis, leading to 'six worlds' comprising Esping-Andersen's 'three-world' typology and three additional CEE worlds as follows:

✓ Former-USSR type (Bulgaria, Croatia, Czech Republic, Hungary, Poland and Slovakia)

✓ Post-communist European type (Bulgaria, Croatia, Czech Republic, Hungary, Poland and Slovakia)

✓ Developing welfare states type (Georgia, Romania and Moldova).

CEE's welfare regimes are 'both mutually differentiated and collectively distinct from the Western countries' welfare typology' (Fenger, 2007). Scruggs I., and Allan, J. (2006) 'suggest that decommodification indices are not strong elements of regime classification' (their conclusion appears to be an argument in favour of an extensive approach to welfare state developments when selecting variables for classification).

Moreover, 'there is less evidence of clustering in different 'worlds' that was found in Esping Andersen' study, where a country scoring high on one index tended to score lower on other indices' (Bazant, U. et al., 2009, p. 17, cf. Scruggs and Allan, 2006, p. 21).

Bonoli (1997) also preferred an alternative route, opting for variables that could depict:

> [The] extensiveness of the welfare state (indicated by social expenditures as a proportion of GDP) and the way the welfare state is financed (indicated by the percentage of social expenditures financed through contributions). (Fenger, 2007, p. 8)

Bonoli (1997) arrived at four ideal-types instead of Esping-Andersen's (1990) well-known threefold typology, adding the Southern type (cf. Fenger, 2007; Arts and Gelissen, 2002; Bonoli, 1997).

The literature on comparative studies in welfare state research is still shaped by a quest for an ideal type of welfare state developments. Esping-Andersen's famous three-ideal type marked only the beginning of the 'welfare modelling business', with it being followed by four-ideal typology with the Southern European welfare regime, once neglected in the initial Western model but becoming an integral part of the modelling business. Other neglected worlds of welfare regimes (e.g. the Asian world, the CEE states) have started to catch up with the 'mainstream' in the literature on comparative social policy. Recent theoretical and empirical developments suggest adding complexity to the well-known frameworks of analysis when considering other worlds of welfare regimes. For instance, the world of CEE welfare regimes has been considered as either belonging or converging to Western types or embarking on a distinct trajectory.

Distinct developments and institutional frameworks (cf. Inglot, T., 2008) are aspects which call for a re-specification of welfare regimes in the CEE. This time, the re-specification should be regarded within a rather divergent path. Communism left a profound and, probably, irreversible, mark on welfare state developments in this part of the world. The transition of CEE countries from communism to capitalism accentuated the already diverged pattern of welfare state transformation. Differences leading to a separate typology, as evidenced by Fenger (2007), emerged within cyclical patterns of *expansion and retrenchment* in the development of specific social policies. Inglot, T. (2008) analysed three former CEE communist countries: Poland, Hungary, Czechoslovakia (Czech Republic and Slovakia after 1993) in a period covering almost one century of welfare state development (1919 – 2004).

Inglot (2008) initiated a comparative-historical analysis of welfare regimes in the CEEs, unravelling the uniqueness of the social reality in this part of the world. Inglot rejected a cluster-type approach to welfare regimes, making the case for a 'theoretical model for the study of historical legacies, institutions, and patterns of social policy development and change in East Central Europe' (2008, p. 51).

Classifying welfare regimes still plays a central role in welfare state development in CEE countries. The increased complexity of typological constructs is confirmed by a new range of studies on welfare state developments focused on the 'worlds' in the CEE, initially ignored within the well-known frameworks of Western model.

Klenner, C. and Leiber, S. (2010) used a gender-based approach and arrived at the conclusion that different paths with different effects on genders were taken during the transformation process. They reviewed the classifications of welfare states in the new CEE members of the EU based on the relative income poverty and unequal distribution. Two groups of welfare regimes emerged:

> [The] Baltic states, Poland, Bulgaria and Romania on one
> less well-off side and Czech Republic, Slovenia, Hungary
> and Slovakia on the more well-off side (and in some cases
> much more so than some of the old EU member states).
> (cf. Keune and Steinhilber, apud Klenner, C and Leiber, S.
> 2010)

Kuitto (2016) classified 26 EU member states into five clusters of welfare regimes: *Conservative continental European or traditional Bismarckian cluster,*[1] *Nordic and Anglo-Saxon countries,*[2] *Southern European countries,*[3] *Central and Eastern European countries*[4] and *Mixed Eastern-Southern*

1   Austria, Belgium, Germany, France, Netherlands, Switzerland.

2   Denmark, Sweden, Norway, Finland, the United Kingdom, Ireland, Italy and Portugal.

3   Poland, Slovenia, Hungary, Spain and Greece.

4   Estonia, Slovakia and the Czech Republic.

cluster[5] (cf. Kuitto, K.., 2016). Kuitto's conclusion is that a 'European welfare state does not group according to Esping-Andersen's framework with regard to decommodifying potential of their social security program' (Kuitto, K., 2016, p. 174).

Ferreira, L. V. and Figueiredo, A. (2005) arrived at *two analytical dimensions*: EU *with 14 states* versus EU *with 22 states*. The EU with 14 states (before the 'first wave') is grouped into two clusters of welfare regime worlds: *The Mediterranean world* and '*a comprehensive cluster of all other countries*'. *EU with 22 states* is clustered into:

> [The] Mediterranean countries (Spain, Italy, Portugal and Greece) [that] maintain their position as a separate cluster; Ireland joins the main block of newcomers; and the Czech Republic, Hungary and Slovenia cluster together with the main block of pre- enlargement countries. In this last cluster one can broadly distinguish two branches: one including the classical family of conservative countries plus the Czech Republic, Hungary and Slovenia; and the second one including the Scandinavian countries and the UK.' (Ferreira, L. V., Figueiredo, A., 2005)

Aidukaite, J. (2011) argues that a 'distinct/unified post-communist welfare regime' [emerged] within the EU based on a comprehensive review of literature. Aidukaite arrives at the idea that:

> [The] post-communist countries cannot be placed exactly within any of the Esping-Andersen's welfare state regimes. [...] the research on welfare state development in the CEE region reveals a number of important institutional features in support of identifying the distinct/unified post-communist welfare regime. (2011)

Schubert, K. et al. (eds.) (2009) embarked on a rather inclusive methodological path: 'From a theoretical point of view, it does not matter, if the distinction of clusters is made via proper cluster analysis or in a more "descriptive" manner' (Ibid, p. 15). Schubert (2009) adhered to the opinion that the long-used empirical basis of the typological constructs in welfare typologizing is eroding.

---

5   Romania, Bulgaria, Latvia and Lithuania.

On the contrary, Haggard, S. and Kaufmann, R. R. (2008) argue that 'following Esping-Andersen (1990), specific social policies do not evolve in isolation but cluster together into identifiable complexes' (2008). Nevertheless, Haggard and Kaufmann (2008) opt for a mixed approach to testing variables in the analysis:

> Although we are interested in cross-regional variations, it is also clear that the cases within any given region also exhibit important variations as well, and that these differences provide additional opportunities for testing. (Ibid, 2008)

Žukowski, M. (2009) classified welfare states from the CEE according to a:

> Two-dimensional approach, including both the quantity of welfare provision, that is, the *how much?* dimension (indicator: social expenditure as a proportion of GDP) and its quality, or *how?* dimension, whose indicator is the proportion of contribution-financing as an approximation of the size of the Bismarckian, as opposed to the Beveridge component in a welfare state (Bonoli 1997; for an extension of this typology, see Bambra 2007).

An Eastern pattern combined with a new variety of Eurocentric knowledge seems to emerge in welfare state classifications. Countries from the CEE:

> [Are] often treated as one group – e.g., as 'transition countries', 'transition regimes', or 'Eastern regimes' – and their similarities to the Southern model are stressed (Maydell et al. 2006, Cerami 2006). (Žukowski, M. 2009)

Newly emerged 'transition regimes' or 'Eastern regimes' embarked on a different pattern of developments. It signals a sort of 'betweenness centrality' (Yan, E. 2009) in the welfare modelling business, marking pivotal points in terms of conceptual and empirical developments. While commentators indicated a heterogeneous and still 'transitional' CEEWM (Deacon, 1993), others argued that welfare states in the CEE became either distinct from the Western-types or manifest features of the Western- types as evidenced in the present qualitative synthesis. We now turn from a general CEEWM to cases.

Case selection method

ARRIVING AT PARTICULAR CASES NEEDS A SYSTEMATIC APPROACH TO selecting the literature. A systematic review requires representations/ components (e.g. diagrams, tables etc.) to arrive at a justifiable and defensible synthesis of the literature.

The reviewer aimed to critically explore, evaluate and synthetize a pool of selected relevant studies based on a *search strategy*. A *diagrammatic representation* (See *Diagram 1* – PRISMA) facilitates the visualization of stages involved in the process of searching the literature. Carrying out a search strategy assumes one basic exigency, the inclusion of all relevant studies that fit inclusion criteria. The process of evidencing search criteria used for setting out the scope of search query is facilitated by a diagrammatic representation of inter-connected search flows. The first step within our chosen diagrammatic representation was to identify the databases. Six databases were selected to carry out the search strategy: Social Science Abstracts, Social Science Citation Index, Sociological Abstracts, Sociology, Web of Science and World-Wide Political Science Abstracts. 'How to' search action formed a significant part of search strategy, requiring the identification of the initial pool of studies based on interrogating the selected databases. Furthermore, identifying more selection criteria as well as adopting a snowballing procedure might be required to arrive at the final pool of studies/titles.

Identifying and operating with organizing concepts is mandatory to arrive at justifiable search terms: The 'welfare state regimes' is the core concept and its variations within a broad search string: <welfare state(s)> OR <welfare regime(s)> OR <regime(s)> OR <Esping-Andersen> OR <worlds> OR <cluster(s)> OR <model(s)> OR <Class> OR <Typology> AND terms about countries such as <CEE> OR <Eastern Central> OR <enlarged Europe> OR <post-communist> OR<post-socialist. OR <Visegrad> OR <Baltic> OR <Balkan> OR <EU27>).

Variations of the 'organizing concept' (i.e. 'welfare state regimes') are based on two conditions:

1. *Conceptual*: variations of 'welfare state regimes' are found in the literature, having similar, slightly similar or related meanings:

   - Syntagma as 'welfare regimes' or 'welfare state regimes' have similar meanings; 'welfare states' are compared using 'welfare regimes' (i.e. the concept of 'welfare state' becomes more comprehensible within the conceptual designation of 'welfare regime'); the concept of 'worlds' of 'welfare regimes' has the same meaning with 'welfare regimes' or 'welfare state regimes'.

   - 'Model' is similar to using 'welfare regime' or 'welfare model' or 'model of welfare' (e.g. 'The Scandinavian model of welfare' (Abrahamson, 1999) or 'The Nordic welfare model' (Abrahamson, 2012) designating a certain 'welfare regime';

   - 'Class' denotes a 'type' or 'group' or 'category' (cf. Weber's 'ideal types') or 'cluster';

   - 'Typology' is often used in the literature as Esping-Andersen's 'ideal- types' or 'Three Worlds' Typology' (Barbara, V.) or 'Three Types of Welfare Regimes' or 'The Three Worlds' (Emmenegger, P., 2015);

2. *Geographical coverage*: comparative studies debating welfare realities in the Central and Eastern Europe is focused on European regions and even supra-national entities: e.g.: Eastern Central> OR <enlarged Europe> OR <post-communist> OR<post-socialist> OR <Visegrad> OR <Baltic> OR <Balkan> OR <EU27>.

Several selection criteria adapted from Ferragina, E., Seeleib-Kaiser, M., (2011, p. 4) were applied to arrive at a pool of titles focused on classification and social/ welfare policy approach and quantitative methods (e.g. cluster analysis):

(1)   the use of quantitative methods;

(2)   the analysis of a minimum of 10 countries [...];

(3)   and the presence of a final classification.

A further 796 titles were excluded, leading to 23 titles. The search strategy was narrowed to the following list of inclusion criteria: 12 full-text articles made up

(1)   the use of clustering techniques;

(2)   the analysis of minimum 10 countries, including Western and Central and Eastern European countries;

(3)   the presence of classification.

A full-text assessment was carried out and a further 11 studies were excluded based on the inclusion criteria. the final pool of studies involved in the 'qualitative synthesis'. The following diagrammatic representation (i.e. PRISMA) represents a 'framework synthesis' (Gough, 2012) of stages involved in the execution of search strategy.

Diagram 1 - "PRISMA 2009 Flow Diagram" for Systematic Review

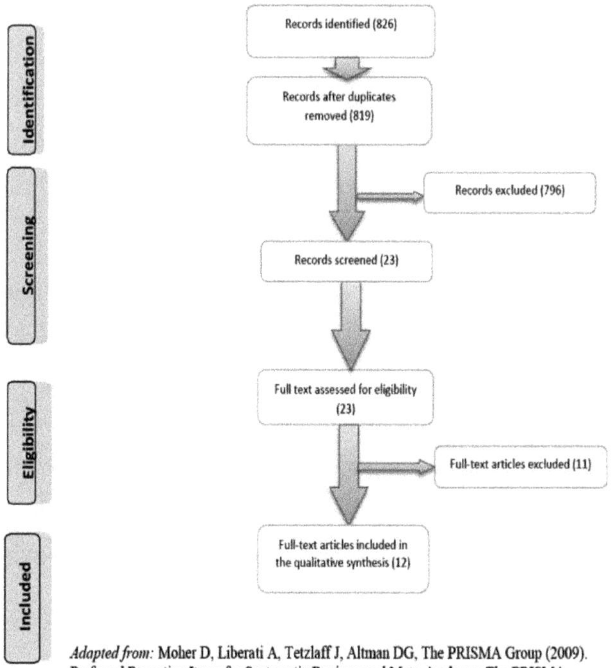

Adapted from: Moher D, Liberati A, Tetzlaff J, Altman DG, The PRISMA Group (2009). Preferred Reporting Items for Systematic Reviews and Meta-Analyses: The PRISMA Statement. Details of selected studies are given below – See Table 1.

Three studies from the final pool of studies exhibit an imprint of 'Three Worlds' typology (Fenger, M., 2007; Castles, F. G., Obinger, H, 2008; Stoy, V., 2014) while three studies arrived at alternative classifications. In terms of composition of classifications relative to the imprint of typological construct, the selected studies arrived at a very mixed 'picture': two classifications, having roots in Esping-Andersen's typology, arrived at a distinct CEE 'world': Fenger (2007) concluded that there are two distinct clusters of CEE countries while Castles, F. and G., Obinger, H. (2008) evidenced that there is a distinct 'post-communist' 'world'. Stoy, V. (2014) argued that there is a distinct group of countries with a rudimentary welfare state [Czech Republic, Greece, Hungary, Italy, Poland, Portugal, Slovak Republic, Spain] although countries such as Greece, Portugal and Spain would rather belong to the Mediterranean type and Italy to the conservative 'world', as they exhibit characteristics that belong to more than one analytical type.

Three studies indicate a departure from the 'Three Worlds' typology, although, this time, the selected CEE region becomes part of 'different' classifications: Kuitto, K. (2016) arrived at a mixed 'picture' of CEE countries clustered in three additional 'worlds', including a 'Mixed Eastern-Southern European cluster'. Ferreira, L. V. and Figueiredo, A. (2005) argued that there is a dominant CEE 'world' (Ireland still joining this group) and a dominant 'Western' 'world' (including three Central and Eastern states). Draxler, J., Van Vliet, Olaf (2010) arrived at a twofold classification: three 'worlds' become two 'worlds'.

The central conclusion is that the CEE welfare states exhibit either hybrid arrangements, followed by arguments in favour of a distinct 'world' and 'other' classifications. In terms of theoretical approaches, three studies are still slanted towards Esping-Andersen's classification while the other research papers exhibit elements in favour of a departure from the 'Three Worlds' typology. The following table summarizes the selected studies based on the theoretical/conceptual frameworks and compositions of the 'worlds'.

Table 1: Countries, 'worlds' of welfare regimes and further classification issues (variables, methods) in selected studies			
Studies	Countries	'Worlds'	Methods/criteria/variables
HJM Fenger (2007)	47 countries: 18 Western states and 29 Central, Eastern European and Central Asian countries	Six worlds (including three CEE 'worlds') comprising Esping-Andersen's 'three-worlds' typology and three additional CEE worlds as follows: Conservative-corporatist type: Austria, Belgium, France, Germany, Greece, Italy, The Netherlands and Spain Social-Democratic type: Finland, Denmark, Norway and Sweden Liberal type: New Zealand, United Kingdom and United States Former-USSR type: Belarus, Estonia, Latvia, Lithuania, Russia and Ukraine Post-communist European type: Bulgaria, Croatia, Czech Republic, Hungary, Poland and Slovakia Developing welfare states type: Georgia, Romania and Moldova	*Hierarchical cluster analysis* Grouping variables based on: *1.Characteristics of governmental programs*: Total government expenditures (average 1998-2003; % of GDP) General health expenditures (average 1998-2003; % of GDP) Government health expenditures (average 1998-2003; % of total government expenditures) Public spending on education (average 1998-2003; % of GDP) Number of physicians per 1000 persons (average 1998-2003) Spending on social protection (% of GDP, 2002 or latest available year) Revenues from social contributions (% of GDP; 2002 or latest available year) Income and corporate taxes (% of GDP; 2002 or latest available year) Individual taxes (% of total government revenues; 2002 or latest available year) Payments to government employees (% of GDP; 2002 or latest available year) *2.Social situation variables* Inequality (GINI-coefficient; 2002 or latest available year) Female participation (% of women in total workforce; average 1998-2003) GDP Growth (average 1998-2003) Total fertility rate (births per woman; average 1998-2003) Inflation (average 1998-2003) Life expectancy (average 1998-2003) Infant mortality (< 5 years, per 1000 births, average 1998-2003) Unemployment (average 1998-2003) *3.Political participation variables* Level of trust (2000)
Kuitto, K. (2016)	10 CEE countries and other E.U. member states	Conservative Continental European or traditional Bismarckian cluster: Austria, Belgium, Germany, France, Netherlands, Switzerland Nordic and Anglo-Saxon countries: Denmark, Sweden,	*Hierarchical Cluster Analysis* along with k-means clustering procedures *12 indicators* grouped as following: Organizational principles of welfare provision: -social contributions as percentage of total social revenue

		Norway, Finland, U.K., Ireland, Italy and Portugal Southern European countries: Poland, Slovenia, Hungary, Spain and Greece. Central and Eastern European countries: Estonia, Slovakia, Czech Republic Mixed Eastern-Southern cluster: Romania, Bulgaria, Latvia, Lithuania	-taxes as percentage of total social revenue -total social revenue as percentage of GDP -contribution revenue as percentage of GDP -tax revenue as percentage of GDP *Policy field emphasis:* -age-related cash expenditure as percentage of GDP (old-age cash benefits + survivors' cash benefits) -working-age income replacing cash expenditure as percentage of GDP (unemployment +sickness + disability + family cash benefits) -health care services expenditure as percentage of GDP (health care benefits in kind) -social services expenditure as percentage of GDP (old-age + family + disability + survivors' + unemployment + social exclusion benefits in kind) *Decommodifying potential:* -replacement rate in different social security programs (sickness, unemployment, minimum pensions) -eligibility criteria in each of the programs (duration of benefits, qualification period required, waiting days) -program-specific generosity indices
Poschl, J., Valkova, K. (2015)	19 European countries	*Cluster 1*: Denmark, Netherlands, Norway *Cluster 2*: Austria, Belgium, France, Germany, Sweden *Cluster 3*: Finland, Greece, Ireland, Italy, Portugal, Spain, United Kingdom *Cluster 4:* Czech Republic, Hungary, Poland, Slovakia	*Cluster analysis and logistic regression* '*Clustering criteria:* › Total public health care expenditures in PPP USD per capita › Inequality in pre-government and post-government equivalent household income expressed as Gini coefficients › Difference between these two Gini coefficients as measurement of overall redistribution effects › Shares of taxes and social insurance contributions in market income › Shares of benefits in disposable income' (Poschl, J., Valkova, K., 2015:118)
Ferreira and Figueiredo (2005)	E.U. 22 states (after the first E.U. enlargement (E.U. 14 + 8 CEE states)	Two analytical dimensions: *E.U. with 14 states* (i.e. the first analytical dimension) grouped into 2 clusters of welfare regime worlds: The Mediterranean world and 'a comprehensive cluster of all other countries' *E.U. with 22 states* (i.e. the second analytical dimension) grouped in three clusters: 'the Mediterranean countries (Spain, Italy, Portugal and Greece) maintain their position as a separate cluster;	*Hierarchical cluster analysis; K-means cluster analysis; Factor analysis* *Dimensions/criteria* used to group 30 variables (set of indicators): *Patterns of welfare provision:* -State, market and family -Public policies and programmes

		Ireland joins the main block of newcomers; and the Czech Republic, Hungary and Slovenia cluster together with the main block of pre-enlargement countries.' (Ferreira & Figueiredo, 2005)	*Welfare outcomes and stratification effects:* -Employment opportunities -Inequality and poverty -Life and education opportunities
Knogler, M., Lankes, F. (2012)	EU-15 and the new EU-10 member states	*5 clusters/'social models':* 1 cluster: BE, DE, NL, AT, DK 2nd cluster: ES, PT, IT, LV, RO, LT, BG 3rd cluster: HU, PL, UK, CZ, IE 4th cluster: EE, GR, SK 5th cluster: FR, SI, FI, SE	*Two-step procedure: Principal component analysis followed by hierarchical agglomerative procedures* *Social policy indicators:* Early leavers from education and training Marginal effective tax rates on employment incomes Reduction of the at-risk-of poverty rate by social transfers Inequality of income distribution Life-long learning Rigidity of employment index Spending on human resources Centralisation and coordination index of wage bargaining Ethics Generosity of unemployment benefits Expenditures an active labour market policy
Puss, T. et al. (2010)	EU-27	Worlds of welfare regimes: *Monetary poverty:* Cluster 1: FR, BE DE, IE, LU, HU, MT, SK Cluster 2: SE, AT, FI, NL, DK, SI, CZ Cluster 3: ES, IT, PT, PL, GR Cluster 4: LT, BG, UK, RO Cluster 5: EE, CY, LV *Public policy:* Cluster 1: FR, DE, AT, BE, NL, ES Cluster 2: SE, FI, DK Cluster 3: PT, GR, BG, IT, MT, PL, UK Cluster 4: SK, HU, LU, CY, SI Cluster 5: LV, LT, EE, RO, CZ	*Two -step analysis, using both hierarchical and relocation clustering methods based on monetary poverty and inequality data. The analysis is based on EUROSTAT data.*
Poder, K., Kerem, K. (2011)	22 countries	Liberals: Portugal, Ireland, U.K., USA, Lithuania, Latvia, Estonia Continentals and Mediterraneans: Spain, Greece, Hungary, Italy, Czech Republic,	*Principal component analysis and cluster analysis* *Variables:* Total government expenditure (% of GDP) Eurostat

		Belgium, Austria, France, Germany, Slovakia, Poland	Health indicators
			LE Life expectancy (years)
		Nordic: Denmark, Sweden, Norway, Finland	IMR Infant mortality rate (per 1,000 births)
			ND Number of physicians (per 10,000 persons)
			HE Government health expenditure (% of GDP)
			Family policy indicators
			FR Total fertility rate (births per woman)
			FRP Female participation rate
			Education indicators
			EE Public spending on education (% of GDP)
			YSE School expectancy (Years of lifetime)
			PTR Pupil-teacher ratio (primary school)
			EPR Participation rate in education, age 15–24 (students as a % of corresponding age
			group)
			Labor market indicators
			U Unemployment rate (% of labor force)
			LU Long-term unemployment (% of total unemployment)
			ER Employment rate (%)
			TU Relevance of labour unions (% of employees in trade unions)
			Social protection indicators
			GINI Gini coefficient (from 0 to 1)
			PR Poverty rate (after taxes and transfers) (60% of median income)
			ISR Income share ratio (80/20)
			SE Government expenditure on social protection (% of GDP)
Castles, F. and Obinger, G. (2008)	20 advanced OECD nations and 25 EU countries	*'Patterns of public policy (1960-1975)'*: • Continental • Nordic • New World • Southern Europe *'Patterns of public policy (early 2000s)'*: • English-speaking • Scandinavian • Continental: 'South' and 'North'	*Cluster analysis* of: (1) cross-national public policy outcomes for the period from 1960 to 1975; (2) public policy patterns at the turn to the twenty-first century *Variables*: Total fertility rate; Employment public sector; Social security contributions; Direct taxes; Indirect taxes; Inflation; Unemployment; Education expenditure; Subsidies; Male employment; Social transfers; Total tax revenues; Female employment; Outlays of government; Economic growth

		'The origins of Public Policy Patterns (1945 – 75)': • Scandinavian • Continental • English-speaking *'Cluster Origins (1985 – 2004)'*: • Nordic • Continental • Southern Europe • English-speaking *'Patterns of Public Policy in the EU-25 (2000 – 2005)'*: • Post-communist': Estonia, Latvia, Lithuania, Hungary, Slovenia, Poland, Slovakia • Nordic • English • Continental	
Burlacu, I (2007)	Moldova and Romania compared with EU-25 member states	8 clusters: Cluster (1): France, Sweden, Germany, Netherlands Cluster (2): Denmark, Finland, Belgium, Luxembourg Cluster (3): Portugal, UK, Spain Cluster (4): Czech Republic, Slovakia, Hungary Cluster (5): Estonia, Lithuania, Lithuania Cluster (6): Cyprus, Malta, Poland, Latvia Cluster (7): Greece, Italy, Austria Cluster (8): Romania and Moldova	Hierarchical cluster analysis Indicators: expenditure on social protection as % GDP; expenditure per capita PPS
Draxler, J., Van Vliet, O. (2010)	25 EU member states	Two clusters: Cluster of new member states Cluster of old member states	Hierarchical cluster analysis Aggregate and disaggregate data on social expenditures on several policy areas (i.e. healthcare, incapacity-related benefits, old age, survivors, family, unemployment, housing and social inclusion)
Lobato, I. R., et al. (2013)	30 of the 32 ESPON countries (i.e. excluding Croatia and Lichtenstein)	Cluster 1: 'Inclusive Centre': Austria, Cyprus, Czech Republic, Germany, Luxembourg, Malta, Slovenia, Switzerland Cluster 2: 'Competitive North-West' Belgium, Denmark, Finland, France, Iceland, Ireland, Netherlands, Norway, Sweden, United Kingdom Cluster 3: 'Disparate East' Bulgaria, Estonia, Hungary, Latvia, Lithuania, Poland, Slovakia	Hierarchical cluster analysis Four 'domains of social exclusion': (1) earning a living, (2) access to services, (3) social environment and (4) political participation Additionally, 'three indicators on which the EU Poverty Target is based on were additionally integrated in the cluster analysis: (1) at risk of poverty, (2) severe material deprivation and (3) jobless households.'

		Cluster 4: 'Mediterranean Crisis' Greece, Italy, Portugal, Spain Cluster 5: Romania	
Stoy, V. (2014)	25 – countries	*Worlds of welfare services*: liberal [Australia, Canada, Finland, France, Iceland, Ireland, New Zealand, U.K.], conservative [Austria, Belgium, Germany, Netherlands, Switzerland, USA] and a social democratic welfare regime [Denmark, Norway, Sweden] and countries with a rudimentary welfare state [Czech Republic, Greece, Hungary, Italy, Poland, Portugal, Slovak Republic, Spain]	Cluster analysis *Dimensions of welfare services*: quantity of services, kind of services, provider of services, payer of services

Expanding the 'Worlds'

ESPING-ANDERSEN WAS CONCERNED WITH VARIATIONS OF WELFARE regimes across boundaries, advancing his regime-type classification and forming the new basis of welfare capitalism. He categorised 'welfare-state variations' (Esping-Andersen, G., 1990, p. 26) by regime types, based on the *criteria of de-commodification, welfare-state stratification* and the '(neglected) *welfare mix*' (Powell, M., Kim, Ki-tae, 2014, p. 628). The 'regime literature' still relies on Esping-Andersen's three dimensions. Such 'a priori theoretical dimensions [...] [can] serve as conceptual lenses or as a "yardstick"' (Ebbinghaus, B., 2012, p. 2) for reviewing our set of selected studies. Esping-Andersen's 'index of decommodification' is 'an essential normative goal of social policy [...], it is, probably, the most frequent used or referred to index in the literature [...]' (Scruggs, L. A. and Allan, J. P., 2003, p. 3).

The authors of selected studies looked at the de- commodification potential through multiple conceptual 'lenses' revealing, that there is an 'extensive' approach to welfare states indicated by social expenditures and 'the way the welfare state is financed' (Fenger, M., 2007; Kuitto, K., 2016). Others employed 'proxies' by constructing a 'reverse scale' (Poder, K. and Kerem, K., 2011). A much broader perspective is noticed at Ferreira and Figueiredo (2005) who opted for a 'very wide conceptual approach: welfare mix, stratification effects and welfare outcomes.' (Arcanjo, M., 2006, p. 27),

54

resembling Esping-Andersen's first (1990) and later dimensions (1999). Widening our conceptual representation of welfare realities strengthens the articulation of the state, market and family, the three 'pillars' forming the 'inter-causal triad' (Powell,2011, p. 86) upon which the concept of welfare regime depends.

Esping-Andersen 'has brought the notion of the welfare mix more centre-stage in his 1999 book' (Powell, M. et al., 2004, p. 86), opening the debate on a more 'radical conceptualization and broadening of focus from "welfare state regimes" to "welfare regimes"' (Gough & Sharkh, 2010, p. 2).

Another expanded version of the welfare mix (i.e. incorporating ALMP – active labour market policies) is empirically evidenced within a cluster analysis of the developed 'worlds' of welfare regimes, becoming an 'updated' version of a mix focused on challenging the 'Three Worlds' through the 'Western lens': Powell and Barrientos (2004) clustered the selected cases, validating the three regimes of Esping-Andersen (1990) 'although with some differences in their composition' (Arcanjo, M., 2009, pp. 7-8).

Poder, K. and Kerem, K. (2011) continued the 'tradition' of using proxies in welfare typologizing by constructing scores of 'commodification' and 'social protection' based on a 'reverse scale (i.e. decommodification score = 1 – commodification score)'. The commodification 'indicates how market-oriented labour policies are.' (Ibid, p. 70) The commodification potential resembles the 'active labour market policies' (ALMP) as a 'key variable' included in the welfare mix (Powell, M., Barrientos, A., 2004) or another indicator that would 'conversely combine labour market flexibility with a low level of income and employment security […].' (Poder, K. et al., 2011, p. 70) The 'commodification' dimension is 'hanging' between two conceptually different dimensions: their justification for commodifying potential could be regarded as pertaining to either welfare mix or decommodification based on a 'reverse scale' (Poder, K. et al., 2011).

Reviewing the selected literature revealed not only a re-conceptualization of selected welfare dimensions but a tendency towards a narrowed perspective in terms of either conceptual dimensions or selection criteria. Jor instance, J. Draxler arrived at a set of 'ten social spending variables and one policy setting variable' (Draxler, J., 2010, p. 127) within the dimension of public policy. Is the CEE 'regime literature' still heavily slanted towards 'conceptual framework and core components developed within a Western context' (Powell, M. et al. 2014, p. 628)? An incongruent perspective in terms of conceptual dimensions can be noticed so far: The 'Western lens' (Hudson and Kühner 2012) appears to be changed, although the dimensions are still slanted towards Esping-Andersen's conceptualization.

Moreover, the representative cases found in the literature, mainly 'hybrid' and 'distinct' 'worlds' are indicators of 'real types' or 'normal types', using Tönnies' concept of 'Normal type'. The sociological notion of 'ideal type' pertains to regime typology. The 'normal type', in this context, suggests the concrete manifestation of welfare regime. Hybridization, for instance, is an example of 'real' type, having characteristics belonging to more than one analytical type.

The discussion now takes on various facets of either 'hybrid' or 'distinct' world as spotted in the literature.

'Hybrid' 'Worlds'

THE CONCEPT OF HYBRIDIZATION GAINED MOMENTUM IN THE welfare modelling business in the CEE region: '[...] an increasing assimilation to Western welfare state archetypes is observable, but the CEECs do not follow one single example' (Hacker, B., 2009, p. 1).

Countries from the CEE cluster within hybrid arrangements, showing overlapping features of the well-known welfare worlds. Kuitto, K. (2016), for instance, grouped Hungary, Poland and Slovenia in the cluster of 'Southern European countries' along with Spain and Greece. A hybrid type tends to combine elements of the CEE welfare states with welfare characteristics rather belonging to Western types. Stoy, V. (2014) pointed out a 'rudimentary welfare state' [Czech Republic, Greece, Hungary, Italy, Poland, Portugal, Slovak Republic, Spain] distinct from the Western 'worlds of welfare services' (Stoy, V., 2014) although, in this case, countries belonging to a 'familistic welfare capitalism' (Papadopoulos, T. et al., 2013)

(Greece, Portugal, Spain and Italy) mix with CEE countries, once more signalling a hybrid arrangement. Other 'arrangements' depict distinct 'worlds', with CEE countries belonging to distinct clusters.

Distinct 'Worlds'

ACCORDING TO CASTLES, F. G., OBINGER, H. 'A STILL MORE distinctive post-Communist family, with clearly defined Baltic and Eastern European sub-types [joined] all the previously existing families of nations' (2008, p. 339). In terms of composition of classification, a 'post-communist' cluster, comprised of Estonia, Latvia, Lithuania, Hungary, Slovenia, Poland and Slovakia, joined the other three groups ('Nordic', 'Continental' and 'English') within the identified 'patterns of public policy in the EU-25' (Castles, F. G., Obinger, H., 2008). Draxler, J., Van Vliet, Olaf (2010) concluded that 'Europeanization might be prevailing over path dependence of distinct models. [...]' (2010, p. 115). However, there is 'a certain deviation from the model — the post-communist new member states (NMS) form a distinct group' (Ibid, p. 115) Fenger (2007) incorporated the Central and Eastern European countries into an expanded typology. He arrived at six worlds of welfare regimes (including three new CEE 'worlds').

Reviewing the selected literature revealed a 'chameleon' CEE welfare regime like the Korean type (Powell, M., Kim, Ki-tae, 2014). The CEE welfare states are clustered in real rather than ideal types. The research on welfare realities in the CEE is still in its infancy as it is not fully settled in terms of arriving at a typology similar to Esping-Andersen's 'Three Worlds'. It is still not clear whether Esping-Andersen's dimensions could be regarded as 'conceptual *lenses* or as a "yardstick" for empirical analysis' (Ebbinghaus, 2012, p. 2) of welfare realities in the CEE. A change of strategy and concepts is needed to cope with an 'unsettled' CEE welfare modelling.

Reviewing welfare realities in the CEE revealed a still unsettled debate, at least in terms of arriving at a unified picture of welfare regimes configurations. The welfare states in the CEE bear the imprint of conceptual and methodological features which are interwoven to form a divergent pattern. The knowledge of CEE welfare realities is still not settled in terms of arriving at a congruent perspective. One possible reason is that either the Western welfare state theories are not firmly rooted, or such theories need to be adapted to CEE realities. One way or another, the researcher needs to understand conceptual frameworks advanced by Western comparative social policy literature.

CHAPTER III

META-ANALYTICAL APPROACHES
TO WELFARE THEORIES

THE COMPARATIVE LITERATURE ON THE DEFINITIONS AND TYPOLOGIES of welfare regimes is far from being coherent. Instead, it is fraught with contradictions. A meta-analytical approach reveals new insights into the nature of welfare state. The contribution of this chapter is twofold. First, it deals with the degree of differentiation in regimes. What case can be made for expanding the Western ideal types? Second, it proposes a meta-analytical approach to various degrees of differentiation by reviewing two meta-analyses (Ebbinghaus, 2012; Ferragina and Seeleib-Kaiser, 2011). Esping-Andersen's typology (1990) appears to be challenged by a variety of 'impure' cases, leading to the question of whether it is an ideal or an influential classification. Comparing consistencies of categorizations reveals a new comparative dimension of welfare regimes.

A meta-analytical approach to welfare classifications reveals relatively different empirical situations and concepts. Therefore, the researcher needs to carry out 're-categorization' by the use of former analytical constructs. The critical issue in the reconstruction of typologies consists in fitting the heterogeneous empirical situations with the logical 'purity' of ideal types. Any typology seems to be rooted in what is usually called an *initial case*. Esping-Andersen's 'Three-Worlds' typology has become 'the starting point for a whole academic industry' (Abrahamson, 1999), although studies arriving at ideal-types of welfare states have received criticism regarding the 'robustness of welfare state models' (Arts and Gellisen 2010, p. 575).

> First, his typology has at least some heuristic and descriptive value, but a case can be made for extending the number of welfare state regimes, perhaps to four or even five, [...] Secondly, these analyses support Esping-Andersen's assumption that there are cases which come close to his three ideal typical regimes, but that there are no pure cases. Some cases are (much) more impure than others [...] (Ibid, p. 577)

The debate on classifying welfare states in ideal-types dates to early 1950s (Abrahamson, 1999) although the discussion took off after the publication of *Three Worlds of Welfare Capitalism* (1990).

Esping-Andersen's comparative studies on welfare state regimes (1990; 1994; 1996; 1999) appear to be disconnected in terms of their developed argumentation in favour of one typology or another: Esping-Andersen spotted additional trajectories with countries from South America and East-Central Europe, broadly matching the characteristics of a liberal regime. Nevertheless, he did not 'incorporate' the new countries and the new trajectories (i.e. 'models that deviate markedly from existing welfare states' (Esping-Andersen, G., 1994, p. 18)) within a new methodological justification apart from a survey of studies:

> Are the nations of East Asia, East-Central Europe or Latin America in the process of emulating the Western model, or are they following qualitatively new trajectories? If by 'new' trajectories we mean models that deviate markedly from existing welfare states, the answer to the second question is essentially 'no'. Our survey does suggest, however, the makings of distinct trajectories that do not necessarily correspond to regional clusters (Ibid)

Esping-Andersen's assertion leaves the door open to further

clarifications. It is not clear, for instance, if 'regional clusters' mean new distinct 'worlds' of welfare regimes. The makings of distinct trajectories could indicate that welfare states in the East Asia, East- Central Europe or Latin America are going to emulate key characteristics of the Western ideal-types. The debate navigates the unsettled terrain of an expanded 'world' of welfare states.

A still unsettled 'welfare modelling business'

THE COMPARATIVE LITERATURE ON WELFARE STATES IS MAINLY rooted in analytical constructs that, 'deliberately, accentuate certain characteristics' (Smith, 2002). Such analytical constructs led to typologies, still bearing the imprint of Esping-Andersen's seminal work (1990).

> Are typologies ideal-type constructs based on analytical concepts or are these only real-type categorizations that summarize cross-national variation of a selected group of countries? (Ebbinghaus 2012)

Answering this question demands further conceptual clarifications. First, "the key characteristic of a typology is that its dimensions represent concepts rather than empirical cases." (Smith, 2002) Esping-Andersen's threefold classification (1990) arrived at three "worlds" of welfare capitalism by recourse to conceptual dimensions. Classification, on its turn, could have cases which do not fall fully within the existing ideal constructs. For instance, a hybrid type is a case which shares features of more than one analytical type. One difference between typology and classification is that arranging in classes based on conceptual dimensions produces categories, i.e. a generalizable representation of something whereas classifying based on empirical evidence could produce empirical cases.

W. Arts and J. Gelissen (2002) '"settle affairs [...] by giving an overview of what [they] think is the gist of the discussion, by weighting the most important arguments and taking stock of the modelling business' (Ibid) Are the 'worlds of welfare capitalism' ideal-types or real- type categorizations? The real-type regimes 'exhibit hybrid forms' (Ibid): 'There are no one-dimensional nations in the sense of a pure case.' (Ibid) Ebbinghaus' 'own calculations and coding (2012) based on Esping-Andersen (1990, 1999)' revealed such hybrid scenarios. Austria originally considered to be a hybrid case belonged to Esping-Andersen's initial Continental and Social-democratic groups (1990). Later, Esping-Andersen (1999) included Austria in the cluster of Continental regimes. Ireland is also considered a hybrid case (Liberal (dominant)/Continental), according to Ebbinghaus' categorization (2012), along with Belgium, Finland, Japan and Switzerland. A meta-analysis of comparative studies on welfare regimes reveals not only a variety of classifications but a dynamic of welfare state variations. Welfare regimes are too static in terms of reflecting historical processes. Ebbinghaus' meta-analytical approach reveals different degrees of consistency of categorization. Hybrid arrangements exhibit 'not much consistency, such as Finland and the Netherlands [which] are very hybrid mixes of several regime types' (Ebbinghaus, 2012). The composition of various classificatory dimensions matters.

The power of classification

KLUGGE, S. (2000) OPENS THE DEBATE FOR AN EMPIRICALLY GROUNDED construction of types and typologies in pseudo-quantitative social research. The 'concept of types' (Ibid) and the 'process of typology construction' (Ibid) need further clarification in the 'welfare modelling business' (Abrahamson, 1999). Marradi (1990) makes a distinction between classification, typology and taxonomy. Is Esping-Andersen's theoretical and empirical framework of the *Three Worlds of Welfare Capitalism* (1990) an 'intentional classification', 'extensional classification' or 'classing' (Ibid 1990)? The 'usefulness of identifying' (Powell and Barrientos, 2011) the 'ideal classification' (McKelvey, 1982) has been neglected.

The 'ideal type' prevails in the literature of comparative welfare state research. There is, also, a tendency to use 'ideal- typical' constructs as a more nuanced version of 'ideal type'. Nevertheless, 'the growing sophistication of welfare state typologizing has left us in a position where the number of categories applied to, and the number of nations in Europe are approximating to each other.' (Deakin et al., 2004)

The overreliance on ideal-types could lead to misclassified cases, as Scruggs and Allan (2006a) warned:

> Relying on the same characteristics as the original decommodification index, our results suggest a very different ordering and clustering of countries. Based on our analysis, the previous results misclassified almost half of the cases.' (Scruggs and Allan 2006a, p. 69)

A misclassification reflects a typological bias in terms of accounting for longitudinal perspectives. Bambra (2006) noticed a 'slight decrease in average total decommodification from 27.2 in 1980 to 25.7 in 1998/99' (Bambra, 2006, p. 79 cited in Schubert, K. et al., 2009) leading to a change of the composition of initial Esping-Andersen's classification (1990).

Scruggs and Allan (2006a) challenged the validity of Esping-Andersen's initial variables (i.e. de-commodification and stratification). Firstly, re-calculated values of stratification and de-commodification indices reveal a different classification as compared to the 'Three Worlds' typology.

A rather mixed picture emerged with countries scoring high in one index not necessarily scoring lower in another index (cf. Ibid). Nuances of liberalism and conservatism were traced:

> Among the traditionally social democratic countries, while more 'liberal' countries (Canada and, to a lesser extent, the UK) also score very highly on the socialism index. Similarly, conservative Austria also places higher on our socialism index compared to the Three Worlds index. (Scruggs and Allan, 2006b, p. 21)

The composition of Esping-Andersen's classification (1990) does not reflect 'pure' types in its entirety.

New analytical approaches like Ebbinghaus' meta-analysis (2012) could bear on new dimensions of comparability. The power of creating classificatory dimensions is challenged by conceptual as well as case selection issues. Comparing classifications could also reveal a misleading overreliance on ideal types. New artificial constructs are needed for the exploration of the existing and new research trajectories.

TABLE 2. Comparing meta-analyses based on selected comparative studies

		Ebbinghaus (2012) 13 selected typologies Consistency		Ferragina & Seeleib-Kaiser (2011) 23 selected typologies Consistency	
		N	(%)	N	(%)
Continental	Germany	10	77%	21	91%
	Austria	9.5	79%	14	82%
	France	12	100%	21	95%
	Belgium	6.5	59%	16	73%
	Italy	8	73%	12	63%
	Spain	3	60%		
	Portugal	2	67%		
	Greece	1	33%		
	Czech Republic	1	100%		
Liberal	Australia	9	69%	15	71%
	Canada	12	92%	15	79%
	United Kingdom	7.5	58%	18	78%
	United States	13	100%	20	100%
	New Zealand	6	55%	9	60%
	Ireland	4.5	45%	10	53%
	Japan	5.5	55%	9	64%
	Switzerland	4.5	56%		
	Iceland	1	100%		
Social-democratic	Denmark	13	100%	20	91%
	Norway	13	100%	20	95%
	Sweden	13	100%	22	100%
	Finland	6.5	54%	12	67%
	Netherlands	5	42%		
Central and Eastern Europe	Estonia	1	100%		
	Hungary	1	100%		
	Latvia	1	100%		
	Lithuania	1	100%		
	Poland	1	100%		
	Slovenia	1	100%		
	Slovak	1	100%		

Sources: Ebbinghaus (2012) based on Esping-Andersen (1990, 1999) and 11 studies cited in Arts & Gelissen (2010), CEE countries (incl. Czech Republic) covered only in Castles and Obinger (2008); Ferragina & Seeleib-Kaiser' (2011); own compilation

Emergence of new research trajectories in welfare classification: new heuristic devices

Ebbinghaus argued that the 'consistency of categorization is perfect or relatively high in the case of some prime cases: in particular Sweden (also Denmark and Norway) as Social Democratic welfare state and the USA as the Liberal model [...]' (Ebbinghaus, B, 2012, p. 6). Such 'prime cases' are just a few (i.e. only four) compared with 18 OECD cases used by Esping-Andersen (1990). Comparative research uses *prime cases* and *prototypes* as real cases approximating analytical constructs. Ideal types are arrangements of welfare state variations. K. Anderson argues that Germany, for instance, is a 'prototype of Esping-Andersen's conservative welfare state' (Anderson, K., 2001, p. 7). Sweden is a prototype of the social-democratic welfare regime (cf. Ibid).

> [...] prototypes [are] countries with welfare state arrangements that very closely relate to the structures of the identified ideal types. (Ferragina, E. and Seeleib-Kaiser, M., 2011, p. 585)

Only three 'prime cases' were identified (cf. Ebbinghaus, B., 2012) when attempting to assess the consistency of categorization in comparative studies, adding to an already 'confused debate' (cf. Ferragina, E. and Seeleib-Kaiser, M., 2011) regarding the representativeness of ideal types in welfare theory development. The debate has been confirmatory rather than exploratory. Reviewing comparative literature on welfare state developments reveals a meta-analytical perspective. A meta-perspective is a collective view of comparative studies. The social researcher needs to go beyond the analytical construct of one typology or another.

Meta-analysis deals with finding patterns by comparing conclusions from different studies. It is a systematic review which, in the case of comparative social policy, leverage the debate on the classification issues in welfare theory developments. Ebbinghaus' meta-analysis (2012) is based on the three classifications in Esping-Andersen (1990, 1999) and the eleven further studies discussed in Arts & Gelissen (2010). A similar meta-analysis was undertaken by Ferragina and Seeleib-Kaiser (2011), covering some 23 studies, with similar results despite the larger sample of studies (Ebbinghaus, 2012, p. 5).

Using meta-analytical dimensions clarifies the robustness of one welfare state model or another but, also, draws attention on the 'consistency of categorization'.

A review of welfare typologies reveals multiple analysing dimensions constituting different 'worlds' of welfare regimes. Each 'world' reflects a typological construct of welfare realities. Esping-Andersen's typology reveals one such 'world': a 'world' of welfare capitalism rooted in the analytical construct of ideal types. Each typological construct is a way of depicting realities, based on a set of indicators/dimensions. De-commodification and stratification form a set of indicators. Bonoli, G. (1997) uses two conceptual dimensions: Bismarck and Beveridge models along with the 'quantity of welfare state expenditure' (Pierson, C., Castles, F.G., 2006, p. 179) leading to classifying welfare regimes in four 'worlds' (British, Continental, Nordic and Southern). Korpi and Palme (1998) classify welfare regimes in five types of welfare regimes (e.g. 'Basic Security', 'Corporatist', 'Encompassing', 'Targeted' and 'Voluntary State Subsidized') considering three dimensions: 'bases of entitlement', 'benefit principle' and 'governance of social insurance programme'.

Grouping comparative social policy studies according to the number of regimes identified unfolds 'three-plus [...] ideal-typical worlds of welfare capitalism' (Arts, W., 1975) as following:

> ✓ three-world typologies (cf. Arts and Gellisen, 2010; Powell and Barrientos, 2004; Bambra, 2006; Scruggs and Allan, 2006);

> ✓ four-world classifications (cf. Arts and Gelissen, 2002; 2010; Shalev, 1996; Vrooman, 2009; Schroder, 2009; Saint-Arnaud and Bernard, 2003; Leibfried, 1992; Castles & Mitchell, 1993; Siaroff, 1994; Ferrera, 1996; Bonoli, 1997; Kangas, 1994; Ragin, 1994);

> ✓ five-world typological constructions (cf. Arts and Gelissen, 2002; 2010; Bambra, C., 2007; Obinger and

Wagschal, 1998; Pitzurello, 1999; Bambra, 2005; Korpi
& Palme, 1998; Castles and Obinger, 2008).

Each typological construct is a variation of Esping-Andersen's 'Three Worlds', extending 'the range of countries included in the analysis' (Bambra, 2007). Variations in the composition of classifications weaken the analytical scheme of an ideal type. The analytical construct cannot be abstracted from experience unless variations of welfare state developments are combined to form an ideal type which is conceptually independent of variables. The comparative literature indicates a variety of ideal types, contradicting the imperative of the independence of variables. Variations in typologies suggest that the analytical constructs are variable-dependents. For instance, a 'minimalist approach is combined with Confucian social ethics' in the case of a 'Confucian welfare state regime' (Bambra, 2007). Another example of a varied type was signalled by Castles and Mitchell (1993) in the case of UK, Australia and New Zealand which 'constitute a Radical, targeted form of welfare state' (Bambra, 2007), departing from Esping-Andersen's ideal construct. There are types of variables we are using in the analysis of welfare state realities. The literature confirms that the range countries varies with the nature of variables included in the comparative analyses.

This chapter intends to review two meta-analyses of welfare state models, those of Ebbinghaus, B. (2012) and Ferragina and Seeleib-Kaiser (2011). One of Ebbinghaus' methodological questions remains: *Are typologies ideal-type constructs based on analytical concepts or are these only real-type categorizations that summarize cross-national variation of a selected group of countries?* (Ebbinghaus, B., 2012) Answering this question could solve the problem of using ideal types in comparative social policy:

> [...] the comparative welfare state research community has largely accepted the benefits of using ideal types and typologies as heuristic devices, as evidenced by the high number of references to Esping-Andersen's seminal work. (Ferragina and Seeleib-Kaiser, 2011, p. 585)

Advancing on a research path focused on meta-analysis of comparative studies evidence reveals rather neglected geographical areas of welfare regimes. On the other hand, it also reveals the attempt to go beyond the boundaries of Western types. A meta-analysis proposes a new perspective in the comparative literature beyond the confirmatory bias related to Esping-Andersen's typology. A meta-perspective on welfare state developments reveals various degrees of consistency of categorizations.

'Consistency of categorization' – a new heuristic device (in meta-analysis)

THE CONSISTENCY OF CATEGORIZATIONS EVIDENCE SIMILARITIES AND differences when comparing the existing comparative literature with Esping-Andersen's welfare state model. Ebbinghaus (2012) and Ferragina & Seeleib-Kaiser (2011) evidenced 'pure cases' or 'prime cases' when the categorization of a certain country in a cluster of regime-type is consistent with Esping-Andersen's ideal type. Ebbinghaus (2012) argued that Sweden, Denmark, Norway, USA are 'prime cases' or countries that are perfectly or very high consistent with Esping-Andersen's ideal categorization.

A comparative analysis of meta-analyses can be focused on two levels of analysis: (1) *comparative tabular data* and (2) *computing techniques*. The first level regards a tabular representation as seen in *Table 3* (above). The information is processed via tabular form, leading to a new representation. Comparing values of consistency of categorization reveals differences and similarities: consistency of categorization is perfect (100%) in the case of France and Czech Republic with continental regime in Ebbinghaus' meta-analysis whereas France (95%) and Germany (91%) are relatively high in the same category in the case of Ferragina & Seeleib-Kaiser's meta-analytical approach (2011). Consistency of categorization is perfect with USA case (Liberal regime) (Ferragina & Seeleib-Kaiser, 2011) while the cases of USA and Iceland are perfectly consistent with Liberal regime in Ebbinghaus' meta- analysis. Three Nordic states (Sweden, Denmark and Norway) appeared to be perfectly consistent in the case of Social-democratic regime (Ebbinghaus, 2012) whereas only Sweden is perfectly consistent with social-democratic regime in Seeleib-Kaiser's meta-analytical approach.

The second level of comparative analysis is an in-depth approach to the relatively new debate on consistency of categorization in welfare typologies. Heuristic techniques facilitate the apprehension of various statistical methods. In research methods, computing purity of clustering is a heuristic technique.

The new heuristic approach is based on computing purity of clustering, only that this time, the referential is changed: purity of clustering countries in regime types is replaced with the consistency of categorization. I will compute the purity of categorization by assigning each country belonging to a regime type according to its consistency of categorization.

A meta-analytical approach to classifying welfare regimes reveals new insights into the nature of typological construct. If computing purity reveals the quality of clustering technique, the consistency of various welfare regimes' clustering results may become an indicator of various persistence levels when compared with ideal types.

The new indicator of 'consistency of categorization' deals with such different persistence levels

THE RELATIONSHIP BETWEEN VARIABLES DENOTES THE CLUSTER Γ_I OF cases (studies) where country x belongs to a welfare regime.

Consistency of categorization $(Cc) = (1/Nt) \sum Cc_i$

where:

Cc_i = consistency of categorization in the case of country i

Nt= number of selected typologies

The case of Ebbinghaus' meta-analysis

Thus, the consistency of categorization (Cc) in the case of continental regime

$= (1/13) \times (0.77 + 0.79 + 1 + 0.59 + 0.73 + 0.6 + 0.67 + 1 + 0.33) = 0.0769 \times 6.08 = 0.4929$

The consistency of categorization (Cc) = 0.4846, considering the liberal regime.

When computing the consistency of categorization with a social democratic regime, the result is 0.3046.

When computing the consistency of categorization in the case of the 'three worlds' of welfare regimes, an aggregate value could be derived.

The aggregate value (Cc (aggregate)) = 1.2821 (0.4929 + 0.4846 + 0.3046) (Cc continental + Cc liberal + Cc social-democratic)

The case of Ferragina & Seeleib-Kaiser's meta-analysis

Ferragina & Seeleib-Kaiser (2011), the value of Cc (aggregate) is: 1.1756 (continental)

+ 0.2195 (liberal) + 0.1534 (social democratic) = 1.5485

Comparing levels of consistency of categorizations reveals a still unsettled welfare reviewing business. Studies classifying welfare regimes based on analytical constructs lead to a variety of 'impure' types, requiring a re-specification of analytical constructs. Further evidence is needed to apprehend different review designs. The first level of analysis deals with clarifying the terminology used in different methodologies. The next chapter is a comparative synopsis of different methodologies identified in the comparative literature.

CHAPTER IV

METHODOLOGICAL DIRECTIONS AND CLARIFICATION OF PATH ALTERNATIVES

Tipping the balance:
cluster techniques or alternatives?

Classificatory issues aiming at 'welfare state regimes' as their core concept, have taken centre stage in academia since 1990. When the case for systematically looking at the "temporal aspects of welfare state differentiation' (Danforth, 2010, p. 3) is made, it opens the debate on whether studying welfare variations should rely on clustering regimes within a 'limited time scope' (Ibid), as identified in the selected literature, or rather follow an alternative route with patterns developing over longer periods of time.

Many caveats remain in the welfare modelling business that focus on the CEE area. The first set of limitations pertains to the still insufficiently clarified temporal aspects of welfare state development. The second set of conditionality circumscribe the problems of various configurations of welfare state variations (e.g. distinct/hybrid/converging towards Western types). The analysis goes further with the problems of 'ideal types' versus 'particular worlds', stressing out the selection of methodological path: static with typologies indicating a limited time scope, trajectories within a prevalent method/technique (e.g. cluster analysis) as developed by

Danforth (2010) or trajectories within a historical and institutionalist perspective as suggested by Inglot (2008).

One further debate identified by Powell & Barrientos is that:

> Esping-Andersen (1990) original intention to provide 'ideal types' has been overlooked in favour of a focus on whether specific countries actually represent a particular world. The more fundamental and neglected point is that these worlds may be produced by studies with different concepts and measures. (Powell & Barrientos, 2011, p. 2)

Arriving at congruent methodological perspectives is imperative in welfare theory development. The comparative literature overlooks welfare realities in favour of typological constructs, neglecting the debates on methodological directions. An audit of circumstances, rather than dimensions/variables/methods in the selected literature, could reveal an incongruence in terms of clarifying the trajectories in welfare state variations.

For instance, the review on welfare realities in the CEE (see Chapter II) confirms that the welfare modelling business is 'heavily slanted towards countries rather than worlds as [a] unit of analysis' (Powell and Barrientos (2011, p. 2).

Should we rely on a single method (e.g. cluster analysis) or adopt a mixed approach? The answer is anchored in the examination of methodological circumstances that would tip the balance in favour of one method or another. The next sections focus on a rather descriptive comparative synopsis of methods as identified in the comparative literature, keeping in mind the three different ways in which scholars have looked at worlds of welfare regimes: as typologies (indicating a rather static perspective with limited time scopes), as trajectories (cf. Danforth, 2010) and as patterns of institutional developments (cf. Inglot, T., 2008). The comparative analysis of methodological perspectives will focus on answering the following question: What are the circumstances hinting towards alternative approaches?

Our main approach is still focused on those particularities of research design underpinning CEE realities, as compared to the Western 'world'. The existing comparative studies focused on the CEE area are still marked by 'real-types', although their methodological basis bears the imprint of an 'ideal' representation. It could indicate that the world of welfare regimes in the CEE is still not fully consolidated in terms of concepts and measure. Some authors (e.g. Deacon, 1993) argued that the welfare regimes in the CEE are moving towards Western ideal-types, others show evidence of a hybrid typology (Kuitto, K, 2016) or 'three-plus' 'worlds' (in this last case, the perspective is still anchored in the Western ideal-type (cf. Fenger, 2007)). Their research design is still slanted towards classifying based on cluster techniques. Comparative studies show empirical evidence in favour of exploring such patterns in the data, leading to various ways of comprehending the new welfare realities in the CEE. One further question is whether the selected empirical analyses using cluster techniques arrived at conclusive results in terms of long-term perspectives on welfare realities. Esping-Andersen's welfare regimes proved to be unstable over long periods of time because of its 'limited time scope' (Danforth, 2010):

> The important point to keep in mind is that cluster analysis can be effective in reducing the diversity in the institutional data, and changes over time (Powell and Barrientos, 2004) [...] (Barrientos, 2015, p. 264)

The reductionist argument favours clustering welfare state variations. It is still debatable whether cluster analysis can depict changes over time if looking over longer time intervals. Considering such variations needs either cluster analysis on long-term intervals (cf. Danforth, 2010) or choosing alternative methodological routes (e.g. historical and institutionalist approach). The next section is focused on the evaluation of cluster techniques as reflected in Esping-Andersen's welfare state analyses.

Clustering welfare state variations

ONE QUESTION REMAINS WHEN CLASSIFYING WELFARE REGIMES BASED on cluster analysis: Are such typologies valid in the context of historical and institutionalist variations? Esping-Andersen admits that short-term welfare configurations are shaped by 'frameworks of historical institutionalism that differ qualitatively between countries' (Esping-Andersen, 1990, p. 80). Whether the concept of 'regime' reflects 'circumstances [...], within frameworks of historical institutionalism' (Ibid), is debatable. For instance, laying the political foundation of social-democratic welfare regime, 'is historically indeterminate; [for] the simple reason that none of the social forces that shape it is predetermined' (Esping-Andersen, 1985, p. 26). Esping-Andersen (1985) suggests that the ideology of the Scandinavian regimes could not display itself according to predetermined events. It contradicts one of his later claims that the concept of regime unfolds a historical institutionalist perspective (Esping-Andersen, 1990).

It is still not clear whether short-term welfare state variations fully reflect a long-term perspective on frameworks of historical institutionalism as suggested by Esping-Andersen. The welfare regimes identified by Esping-Andersen (1990, 1999) seem to be unstable over a long period of time (cf. Danforth, 2014; Ferragina, E. et al, 2015).

Esping-Andersen (1990) referred to 'frameworks of historical institutionalism' when explaining the circumstances that caused the concept of welfare regime emerged in the welfare modelling business. Barrientos (2015) spotted the effectiveness of cluster techniques in 'reducing the diversity of institutional data', suggesting a methodological advantage when carrying out a cluster analysis.

Nevertheless, the framework of historical institutionalism needs further clarification. A central idea of historical institutionalism is that institutions develop within a process of juxtaposing different institutional logics. We shall emphasize the difference between the historical institutionalism developed, in time, 'under the broad umbrella of comparative politics' (Landman, T., 2003, p. 2) and the institutional logic (Thornton, P.H. and Ocasio, 1999; Thornton, P.H. et al., 2012; Friedland and Alford, 1991) that is rooted in sociological theories and organizational studies. The historical institutionalist perspective emphasizes the historical developments of institutional orders while the institutional logic is focused on the 'supraorganizational patterns of activity by which individuals and organizations produce and reproduce their material subsistence and organize time and space' (Friedland & Alford, 1991, p. 248). Time and space become dependent variables within historical institutionalism. For instance, frameworks of historical institutionalism reveal not only variations between countries of the CEE region but, also within each welfare state configuration. A particularity of welfare state developments in this part of Europe is their '"emergency" decision-making manner that is strongly linked to economic and political crisis throughout history (Inglot, 2008, and this volume)' (Cerami, A. & Vanhuysse, P., 2009, p. 18). The institutional and policy legacies of the past:

> [Largely] impact on the possibilities of present and future policy making, which in turn result in continuities and recurrent patterns in the development of the East Central European welfare states and politics of social policy. (Goedeme, T., 2009, p. 1317)

Welfare states, at least in the CEE, developed in a cyclical manner where periods of retrenchments alternated with expansions, changing structures of welfare policies and institutions in layers of 'institutional legacies':

> Institutional legacies represent structures and norms that are firmly embedded in the processes of state building and rebuilding during different historical periods. (Inglot, T., 2008, p. 41)

Clustering welfare regimes based on such different historical periods not only requires using dimensions and variables that could reflect structures and norms embedded in the sequential transformation of welfare state development, but foremost a continuous recalibration of dimensions and variables to embed the cyclical pattern of political and institutional change.

> Politics of welfare retrenchment operates according to fundamentally different rules from the politics of welfare expansion [...] (Levy, J. D., 2010)

A historical and cyclical pattern of retrenchment and expansion in the CEE area makes the analysis based on cluster techniques difficult to apply due to 'timing, sequencing, and duration of each period of growth or reform of social policy' (Inglot, T., 2008, p. 307) as well as the availability of data on longer time intervals.

The timing of cyclical patterns of social policy transformations in this part of Europe embeds three consecutive periods: interwar, post-war and post-communist. Inglot considered these three-eras as 'relevant periods of the regime formation and consolidation' (Ibid, p. 306) in East Central Europe. Clustering regimes based on long periods of time requires comparability of data, a condition difficult to attain. One reason is the reliability of data when doing a comparative analysis. Presumably, statistical reports were distorted in communist regimes:

> Many of the figures in the official statistics contain an intentional distortion and are expressly misleading. The gathering of data is obstructed by secretiveness. The continuity of the time series is broken by constant reorganizations. (Kornai, J., 1992, p. 14)

The sequencing of social policy transformations complicates matters when considering clustering welfare regimes over longer time intervals:

> Temporal sequencing of the social insurance programs also appears to have a special significance; the oldest types of benefits, that is, the ones introduced specifically in the interwar period tend to be the most difficult to change and reform. Newer, post-war programs are usually much easier to restructure and change. (Inglot, T., 2008, pp. 313-314)

The dynamics of welfare state developments in the developing countries require further examination of alternative methodological routes. Changing the 'lens' to welfare state developments has become urgent in the comparative literature. Cluster techniques become short-term predictors of welfare dynamics, requiring further conceptual and empirical investigation.

A longer time perspective should be considered within a revised methodological framework. It is not only a matter of when and for how long such welfare regimes emerged over a long-time interval. It is also a matter of explaining the *overlapping features* of welfare programmes over longer time intervals. The developed 'worlds' of welfare state variations fully emerged as ideal-types and the various empirical frameworks produced in the literature need to be congruent (Powell, M. and Barrientos, A., 2011).

The developing CEE 'worlds' of welfare regimes are still moving towards one proto-type or another, calling for proto-types. These are indicative of a distinct process of welfare state developments in this part of Europe. I identified several shortcomings when looking at the dominant methods used in the selected literature. Historical and institutionalist approaches could provide an alternative explanation. The next section focuses on framing such an alternative route.

Hinting towards a dynamic approach in typology business: 'clustering by pattern similarity' versus layering pattern

LOOKING AT THE DYNAMIC OF WELFARE REALITIES IN THE DEVELOPED world, Danforth argued that the *Three Worlds of Welfare Capitalism* 'began emerging by 1975, became more distinct by 1980, and were stable by 1985' (Danforth, 2010, p. 1). A dynamic of welfare state developments in the developed countries is based on the 'role of cumulative incumbency in creating distinct welfare state regimes and the role of weak path dependence in sustaining the discreteness of these regimes' (Ibid).

Much of the attention revealed 'refining and expanding the tripartite classificatory framework to include new dimensions of differentiation and additional worlds of welfare' (Ibid, p. 2):

> With this intense focus on the conceptual and geographical elements of welfare state classification, however, little attention has been paid to the temporal and evolutionary aspects of Esping-Andersen's three welfare state regime types. (Ibid)

The methodological perspectives identified in the selected literature exhibit divergent trends in terms of clarifying welfare state types in the CEE. Nearly all empirical studies hint towards a static perspective. Two divergent methodological routes could be spotted in the selected literature on CEE welfare regimes:

- A dominant methodological route emphasizing methods and dimensions focused on time intervals circumscribing the post-communist era. It is the typological route.

- An alternative and insufficiently explored alternative focused on either trajectory depicted within well-known methodological routes – e.g. cluster analysis over long-term intervals (cf. Ibid) or historical and institutionalist framework (cf. Inglot, T., 2008).

The alternative route indicates a dynamic perspective. Scholars look at welfare realities through the 'lens' of trajectories based on either cluster techniques (cf. Danforth, 2010) or historical and institutionalist frameworks (cf. Inglot, 2008). Comparing the two identified routes shows a divergent and highly unbalanced perspective on welfare state variations in favour of the typological route.

Danforth (2010) opened the debate on comparing welfare regimes in the developed world by clustering worlds of welfare regimes within a longitudinal perspective. Choosing a typological route within a longitudinal perspective could reveal not only the prevalence of one welfare regime or another but, foremost, 'their long-term trajectories' (Ibid, p. 2). Looking at trajectories of welfare state developments reveals a *longitudinal variety of ideal types*. For instance, the worlds of developed welfare regimes identified around 1975 (Ibid, 2010) were different from the ideal-types identified by Esping-Andersen in 1990:

> By looking at the differentiation between welfare states over time in the post-war era, this inquiry shows that a series of subtle but important shifts between 1950 and 1975 preceded the rise of three distinct groups of welfare states. (Ibid, p. 2)

One central idea could be derived from Danforth's analysis: welfare patterns in the developed world 'do not support a strong 'critical juncture' interpretation of welfare state development' (Ibid, p. 16) as opposed to 'abrupt institutional change' (Cerami, A, Vanhuysse, 2009, p. 3) that could explain the 'emergency' nature of welfare state in the Eastern Central Europe (cf. Inglot, T., 2008).

One more question arises from comparing patterns of welfare state developments in Europe over a long period of time: Can we still rely on cluster analysis in the investigation of welfare state developments in the CEE? An attempt to answer this question requires the identification of new conceptual dimensions. The reason is that the welfare realities in the CEE followed a layering development. For instance, the Bismarckian tradition permeated an `emergency` route of welfare developments during the communist era. Such a layering perspective depicts a historical and institutionalist framework. Clustering welfare regimes means arriving at distinct types. How can we determine the distinctive character of a regime when a layering pattern 'derives from different origins [so that] it can also evolve and change independently over time?' (Inglot, T., 2008, p. 43).

> In short, a welfare state that develops in this manner should not be analysed as a teleologically transparent or predesigned sum of all its constituent parts crafted by one particular regime at any given time in history. (Ibid)

Deciding on a course of methodological action requires apprehending alternative routes.

> Can we classify all (European) welfare states within a single parsimonious typology of social policy regimes? (See Esping-Andersen 1990; Tomka 2004) How do we identify and define relevant historical legacies? (See Grzymala-Busse 2002; Ekiert and Hanson 2003b; Kopstein 2003) And what are the mechanisms that transmit these legacies over time? (See Thelen 1999, 2003, 2004; Pierson 2004) (Inglot, T., 2008, p. 307)

How can we arrive at a set of dimensions/criteria depicting welfare realities based on such historical legacies? The problem of arriving at a typological construct in the CEE becomes evident when trying to 'detect the phenomenon of 'permanent construction sites' or 'layered' structuring of social policy institutions, which often incorporate highly inventive combinations of old and new benefit programs.' (Ibid)

Such a 'layered' development becomes difficult to apprehend within cluster techniques. The phenomenon of 'permanent construction sites' rather indicates a dynamic influenced by:

Different origins (beginning stages), timing, and sequencing of the development of social welfare institutions, programs, and policies [that] give rise to distinct varieties of 'emergency' welfare states in East Central Europe. (Ibid, p. 308)

Institutions and programs of welfare states from Eastern Central Europe (Ibid) dating from the 20th century did not cease to exist after 1945, but they entered a process of rebuilding, reconfiguration, unification and expansion (cf. Ibid).

The CEE welfare state developments gained the imprint of a *co-existent welfare state variation*. Institutional frameworks, as well as welfare programs depicting welfare realities in the CEE area, evolved simultaneously. Some welfare state variations were not only spotted as being deeply rooted in the Bismarckian tradition but, also bearing the imprint of a cyclical development of social policies. It indicates that CEE welfare programs entered a layering development during a long period of time marked by a cyclical pattern.

Welfare states in Eastern Central Europe developed in two superimposed structuring layers: one induced by older welfare programs and institutional legacies having imperial roots, while institutional and policy layers were added over a cyclical period of expansion and retrenchment during post-war welfare state developments.

The pattern of welfare state developments in the CEE indicates not only cyclical dynamics but a co-existent transformation of welfare realities. The dynamics of welfare state variations evolved in a co-existent succession of social policy transformations. Inglot's historical and institutionalist approach hints at a co-existent variation. Inglot arrived at a 'typical "communist welfare system" as a combination' of structures or components' (Ibid, p. 26).

Inglot suggests that the identified 'communist welfare system' has imperial roots: Inglot argued that the Bismarckian tradition represented the 'foundations' of the identified 'communist welfare system':

In the interwar period the core group of Eastern and Central European welfare states was built on the foundations established under the German, Hapsburg, and, to a lesser degree (in the Polish case) Russian imperial rule [...]. (Ibid, p. 24)

The Bismarckian tradition became, in time, a tough nucleus for what Inglot identified as being the 'communist welfare system'. One possible explanation for such 'discernible historical foundations' (Ibid, p. 24) rests on what Postolache (2007) called as the 'comprehensibility through a division between a tough nucleus and a specific environment' (Badescu & Badescu, 2014, p. 339).

The tough nucleus is represented by the 'inherited institutional foundations (1880-1915)' (Inglot, T., 2008, p. 25).

The German Social Insurance Law of 1911 and the Austrian Social Insurance Act of 1906 [...] [were] designed for an advanced industrial society with a large, modern bureaucracy [and] were inherited by newly independent eastern countries with underdeveloped economies, weak governments, and impoverished, mostly rural populations [...] (Ibid, p. 24)

The Bismarckian origin of welfare states permeated through almost one century of welfare state developments in the Eastern Central Europe. Inglot (2008) referred to it as the 'historical core of the European welfare states' (Ibid, p. 26) or 'historical core with reinforced earnings-related principles' (Ibid, p. 32). Adopting a historical and institutionalist approach could clarify the dynamics of welfare transformations. There is a '"layered" construction, with old components adjusted and new ones added during different historical periods in a manner reminiscent of geological deposits' (Ibid, p. 43). It lays the foundation for an entirely renovated mode of thinking welfare variations in this part of Europe.

Varieties of welfare state developments in the CEE become difficult to apprehend within a typological construct as welfare realities have different origins, timings and sequencing. There is a variety in emphasizing 'particular types of benefit over time' (Ibid, p. 309):

> In essence, in the Soviet Union from the early days of state-sponsored industrialization, full employment had served as a convenient substitute for underdeveloped social insurance. In contrast, the countries of Central and Eastern Europe had adopted and maintained social insurance as a steady replacement for regular earnings. (Ibid, p. 308)

The timings and the sequencing of varieties of welfare states in the CEE pertain to a process of developing such realities into an 'entity with several layers of institutions and laws, many dating back to the interwar period.' (Ibid, p. 26):

> Without minimizing the importance of various indigenous elements in each country, we can conceive of a typical 'communist welfare system' as a combination of three basic structures or components: (1) the original social insurance institutions and programs, inherited from the previous regimes but rebuilt, reconfigured, unified, and expanded since 1945, (2) post-war additions of the newer 'socialist' institutions and benefit schemes, and (3) the imported, Stalinist model, that is, the Soviet blueprint for the organization, financing, and administration that had been originally designed in Moscow in the 1930s. (Ibid)

It is worth noticing that such a combination of structures or components of welfare states in the CEE stretches over a long period of time, including three consecutive yet inter-twined intervals in terms of their historical and institutionalist development: pre-war period, communist era and post-communist transformations. These intervals are not only sequential, taking place within a certain historical period. These periods are envisioned as belonging to a *successive co-existence* of welfare state developments. Welfare state variations succeeded within long periods of time in a co-existent way. The identified layering pattern (cf. Ibid) indicates a superimposition of institutional frameworks and welfare programs: some of these programs (i.e. 'the oldest types of benefits' (Ibid, p. 313)) permeate through a long historical period of welfare state developments while others (i.e. 'newer, post-war programs' (Ibid, p. 313)) can be structured more easily. It points not only to the 'age of the programs' (Ibid, p. 314) but, also, becomes indicative of a co-existent succession of such welfare programs:

an inherited Bismarckian tradition co-existed with the new programs in a succession of different time intervals characterized by cyclical patterns. The age of the welfare programs becomes not only a predictor of welfare spending but, also, an indicator of a co-existent type of welfare state developments.

> The evolution of humankind was framed within two polar tendencies: simple succession versus co-existent succession. Neo-evolutionist theories make the distinction between the two identified facets: specific evolution and universal evolution. (Badescu, I., 2008, p. 1)

We may argue that welfare state variations developed in history within such identified frameworks (simple versus co-existent succession), given the imprint of the Central and Eastern European welfare 'world'. The welfare regimes in this part of the world become intelligible within the paradigm of regional worlds. Welfare capitalism is not revealed any more as a uniformizing reality but, foremost, as a vibrating reality in the context of regional styles of welfare regimes. Globalization bears the imprint of such regional styles which make welfare state variations more discernible.

PART II
REGIONAL WORLDS

CHAPTER I

THE TRANSITION AND THE WELFARE STATE IN CENTRAL AND EASTERN EUROPE[†]

THE LAST DECADE OF THE TWENTIETH CENTURY WAS A PIVOTAL PERIOD in the history of the welfare state paradigm. The fall of the Berlin Wall, as well as the revolutions in Central and Eastern Europe, dramatically reconfigured the social conditions of these societies. We may agree with Fenger (2007) that there are differences between Central and Eastern European welfare regimes and Western welfare regimes. What are the causes of such differences? Is this evidence of an inability to pursue those required structural changes for re-configuring the post-communist welfare regime according to a Western pattern? Or is this the confirmation of a distinct welfare regime in the Central and Eastern European region? New 'welfare logics' emerged in the post-communist societies. Such an emerging

---

[†]   Resuming a line of argument traced back to my published work (i.e. Badescu, C. (2013) *Fundamentele culturale ale crizelor economice De la etnoeconomie la teoria proprietatii identitare* (Cultural Foundations of Economic Crises From Ethnoeconomy to the Theory of Identitary Property), Bucuresti: Ed. Muzeului Național al Literaturii Române and Badescu, C. (2013) *Some Considerations on a New Typology of Welfare Regimes*, in Zamfir, E., Maggino, F. (eds.), The European Culture for Human Rights: The Right to Happiness, Cambridge: Cambridge Scholars Publishing, pp. 356-367).

process is going on within and through a long-lasting global crisis of the 'modern world system' as Immanuel Wallerstein (1974) called it.

'Transitions' in the Global Context

IS THE 'SYSTEMIC DEFAULT OF THE CAPITALISTIC SYSTEM' (HANUSCH & Wackermann, 2009) the major cause of the actual crisis? Or is it 'rather a consequence of its major success' (Ibid, 2009)? These are two major questions we need to address when trying to explain the causes of the global crisis and of its specification within a regional world like the CEE one. Our attention now moves to those structural features of the capitalist system. We tend to consider the nature of the disequilibrium of the system itself.

The capitalist system reached a point where the structural equilibria of the system was slowly undermined by the advance of financialization of social reproduction. One possible definition of financialization refers to the process through which the mechanisms of the financial sector distort the structural equilibria in the real economy. The spiral of indebtedness has become the 'vehicle' through which our modern society experienced an unprecedented increase of real estate prices. One possible underlying feature that started to become the justification for the advance of an excessive, distortionary financialization, is that real estate became just another asset class for institutional investors:

> Direct ownership of properties has been exchanged into shares of properties, that is, fictitious capital, creating an impetus for 'objectified numbers' to measure the performance of these indirect investments. (Van Loon, J., Aalbers, M. B., 2017)

Sassen, S. (2012) spotted the danger of the advance of such 'fictious capital':

> The particular case of the so-called subprime mortgage crisis can be conceptualized as one instance of systemic expulsion through an extension of an advanced mode of capitalist relations of production – the financializing of non-financial domains. (Sassen, S., 2012, p. 75)

The subprime mortgage crisis has become the epitome of a capitalist system that reached a point of structural disequilibria. We may argue that the capitalist system is always in a dynamic disequilibrium in a Schumpeterian view. The system cannot survive unless the actors involved (e.g. companies) are able to generate 'genuine profit' due to the innovation process. Schumpeter's dimension of innovation within his perspective of 'creative destruction' is the only theory which so far explains why there is something we call 'profit'. Societal evolution was significantly influenced either by so-called 'drivers', like 'creative destruction' (Schumpeter, J., 1942) itself, or by ways in which the state managed to redistribute wealth through taxation: 'Societal evolution was driven ... by the ways in which states tackled the challenges of raising revenues and managing spending' (Moore, 2004). Our question is whether 'genuine profit' due to innovation, in a Schumpeterian view, is socially and ethically desirable. Or is profit the *raison d'être* for the existence of the business?

The analysis is focused on finding out appropriate answers to these fundamental questions. Thus, we need a new theory which integrates explaining society with explaining the economic process which 'consumes' so- called 'order'; in other words, it produces 'entropy,' a key concept originated by Nicholas Georgescu-Roegen (1971). The idea of entropy leads us to a major concept in economy, i.e. 'creative destruction,' explained in Schumpeter's famous work, *Capitalism, Socialism and Democracy* (1942).

Globalization has confronted humankind with new opportunities and new perils. One of the misleading dangers of globalization is the hybridization of cultural features and resultant destruction of multiple cultural identities. While denounced by all theorists, the effect of globalization is gaining despite the price of this destruction, or the 'illness of specificities'.

A second dangerous effect has been denounced by Howard Bloom, which warns of the threat wherein some subcultures take control of the overall perception of humanity.

A cultural foundation of the actual economic crisis must be traced back for centuries, when the tax-states emerged:

The great historical transformation in modern Western European history was neither the emergence of capitalism (Marx) nor the rise of modern rational bureaucracy (Weber), but the transition from the *demesne* (or *domain*) *state*—where government activities were funded from surpluses derived from the rulers own properties—to the *tax state*, that was funded through regularized tax levies on the private sector and private incomes. (Moore, M., 2004)

The crisis that rocked the world's most powerful economies became one of the most terrible challenges for economics. Great world leaders, from the spiritual to political, have concluded that, in its essence, this world crisis is a moral one and its causes should be sought at the level of spiritual foundations.

Therefore, analysis should take place within the framework of the relationship between economy, wellbeing and culture. Economic crises are the most alarming phenomena within the dynamics of human societies. They propagate in a way which affects the entire collective mentality, being pre-announced through what is happening at the level of the spiritual foundations of economies. This matter was investigated by the great economists and sociologists, yet the process of building a theory on the cultural foundations of the economic crises has been delayed.

The delay itself is a part of what we can call the inertia of crisis. The phenomenon is similar to that of the relationship between wars and the processes of organizing peace. Organization of peace begins long before the end of the war, and afterwards, all the energies are concentrated on the process of its establishment. The same happens with the phenomenon of crisis—both during and after their propagation, the minds of politicians are focused on development policy issues, the removal from the crisis and much less on issues such as the crisis itself.

The issue is still more complicated in the context of the mega-process of globalization, which induces massive deconstructions, disproportions, conflicts, anarchy, and a profound identity crisis on the scale of the global system, as it is presented in the theory of peripheralization etc.

The paradigm of cultural foundations of crisis has brought into debate the dimension of *intellectual capital*, as a key factor of competitiveness of economies. Such a consideration will move the field of our analysis towards a more focused approach of the distinctions between the 'take-off' elites and the elites of the crisis, evoking famous theories like Toynbee's theory (on the relationship between the elite and the crisis of civilizations), the take-off model of economic growth (Rostow), the theory of quasi-rent, Schumpeter's theory of innovation and last, but not least, the theory of identity rent (Tudorel Postolache, etc.).

The relationship between the modern world system and the geo-culture of the crisis arising at the ending phase of the civilizational cycle should be re-examined. The question would be whether the modern world system has entered a period of serious disequilibrium based on a series of consecutive systemic failures of the state, along with the systemic change of the institutional arrangements of the modern capitalist system. It led to what Wallerstein called the 'vortex,' referring to that 'vicious circle, in which each failure of the state leads to less willingness to entrust it with tasks' (Wallerstein, 1999, p. 32). A similar vicious circle could emerge in the case of post-crisis developments, in which each further attempt to deal with possible causes of crisis leads to less willingness to entrust major stakeholders (e.g. state, Central Banks etc.) with tasks.

For instance, one recent issue concerns the state of losing grip in promoting optimal macroeconomic performance through monetary policies. Some recent discussions regarding the impact of some central banks' decisions, although limited to a debate in periodical publications, is still open to further debate. The Federal Reserve Bank (i.e. the Central Bank of USA) has reduced its benchmark federal interest rate, a decision preceded by European Central Bank's suggestion that a rate cut could be on the horizon. It confirms that two prominent central banks of the global economy embarked on more monetary policy easing, followed by other easing measures recently taken, or likely to be taken, in emerging markets (e.g. Brazil Central Bank, Central Bank of the Republic of Turkey). We are witnessing a decade of cumulative monetary easing efforts, going back to the 2008 financial crisis. Searching the Internet for keywords like 'central banks' and 'easing' returns 'catchy' 'headlines': 'Global Easing Cycle Gains Momentum as Central Banks Cut Rates' (The Wall Street Journal); 'Central bank watcher: Time to Deliver'; 'Why the European Central Bank is getting ready to cut rates' (marketwatch. com); 'Bank of Japan commits to easing further if inflation sputters, keeps policy steady' (Reuters). The debate around unconventional policies is, indeed, appealing to commentators, and requires some clarifications.

The mechanisms through which central banks purchase bonds deepens inequality. Some recent figures estimate that such unconventional monetary policies benefit the richest families:

> The Bank of England itself estimates that QE boosted bond and share prices by around 20% (Bank of England, 2011). In theory, this should make people feel wealthier so that they spend more. However, 40% of the stock market is owned by the wealthiest 5% of the population, so while most families saw no benefit from Quantitative Easing, the richest 5% of households would have each been up to £128,000 better off (according to Strategic Quantitative Easing, p. 28, by the New Economics Foundation). (Positive Money Europe)

Quantitative easing (QE) deepened inequality by increasing the wealth share of the wealthiest. Central Banks embarked on variety of QE, by pledging to buy a tremendous amount of debt in order to boost growth although 'the empirical analysis indicates that QE [...] had no apparent effect [for instance] on the UK economy.' (Lyonnet, V., Werner, R., 2012)

> Our analysis suggests that the [asset] purchases [of the central bank] have had a significant impact on financial markets and particularly gilt yields, but there is clearly more to learn about the transmission of those effects to the wider economy (p. 4). (Joyce et al., 2010 apud Lyonnet, V., Werner, R., 2012, p. 4)

The transmissions of such policy effects appear as being not only ineffective in terms of a wider economic impact but also in terms of wealth redistribution. QE benefited financial markets by boosting share prices and accumulating wealth for the richest, accentuating disparities of wealth between rich and poor.

All this shows us that globalization does not standardize nor increase the order of the world, but, on the contrary, such a process cannot be thought of as a universal panacea for the world crises of today and tomorrow because of so-called 'transitions' in the global context. These 'transitions' are more equitable with periods of endemic turbulences than with 'emergent structures' that are a regularity of periods of sudden or massive change.

In general, we can say that in any change we must seek a nuclear composition of two opposite and complementary elements: immanent and transcendence, i.e. given elements and super-added elements which, since they are already added over those given elements (already existing) they appear to get special qualities.

Immanence is *the given* of any phenomenon, and transcendences are the superadded qualities at the immanent composition of the phenomenon. These superadded qualities illustrate what economists used to call active intangible assets hard or almost impossible to imitate. If superadded qualities lack or fail to get active in the social composition of transitional process, then we shall confront with an inter-regnum period dominated by turbulences and anarchy.

Economists talk about 'emerging markets,' i.e. about the birth and consolidation of capital markets, for instance, or the stock markets in so-called 'frontier' areas of the system (or frontier markets). The element of the given of that phenomenon is always there, while the 'element' which is superadded might not be always there, so emerging structures have two facets and are structures with an ontological deficit. Therefore, the potential evolution of Eastern societies after the fall of communist regimes was not of that *one-evolutionary* type of process but of a bifurcation type so that Eastern societies appear to have evolved either towards emergent structures or towards turbulent phases. The role of super-added elements was a decisive one for the success of transition, i.e. for the first type of change wherein the emergent structure finally prevailed. If super-added elements failed to become active in the behaviour of the elite, society moved towards a lasting turbulence. On the other hand, as Friedman theory of inflation argues, inflation itself acts as a super-added element so it can prepare a perverse path towards failure. It reveals a factor of 'lock-in potential', as Kominek (2009) argues.

The great challenge is to make the two components ineligible, developing the theory that helps us to address the phenomena through this nuclear dualism, as *donum* and *superadditum*, as what is given and what is super-added. We invoke some famous theories to use them for having access to the new edifice of the new knowledge.

Wallerstein considers that the new system of the world, which he called 'the modern world system' to distinguish it from the world systems of historical Empires, was born through a 'process of transformational [that] had a multilevel character' (Zolberg, A. R., 1981, p. 274). What is curious is that his analysis refers to those elements which make up the *datum* of the phenomenon and those that make up the *super-added qualities* of the central area (core area), and which may explain the 'passionarity impulse' (Gumilev, L., 1978) which gives birth to the system—the same 'passionarity impulse' that would have led to the emergence of so-called 'risk production societies.'

From the 'Wealth Production' to the 'Risk Production Societies'[1]

CONTRARY TO THE INDUSTRIAL SOCIETY, WHERE 'THE SOCIAL production of wealth is systematically accompanied by the social production of risk' (Beck, U., 1992, p. 19) as a side-effect, in the transitional society, the political production of privileges is accompanied by the

---

1 The idea of so-called 'transitions' from the 'wealth production' to the 'risk production societies' was developed in my book *Criză și fiscalitate* [Crisis and Fiscality], (Bucharest: Mica Valahie Publishing House, 2010), where I revealed the phenomenon of indebtedness as a major social risk of today's modern society. I have also used this perspective, i.e. the transition towards 'risk production societies', as a parameter invoked in the analysis of the cultural foundation of crisis that is, also, the subject matter of my postdoctoral thesis within the Postdoctoral School ('Harnessing Cultural Identities in the Globalized Processes') at the Romanian Academy.

political production of risk. In the industrial society, the problems and conflicts relating to distribution in a society of scarcity overlap with the problems and conflicts that arise especially from the production definition and distribution of techno-scientifically produced risk (Ibid). In the post-communist transition society, the same problems and conflicts, related to distribution in a society of scarcity, overlap with the problems and conflict that arise from the political production of privileges. The whole reform seems to be reduced to a regulation of the political mode of redistribution of risks within a given society.

Beck spotted a 'change from the logic of wealth distribution in a society of scarcity to the logic of risk distribution in late modernity' (Beck, U., 1992, p. 19). As to the Eastern European societies, I would call these sorts of risks, which are politically produced and redistributed, 'peripheral risks,' i.e. risks that systematically accompany the situation of living in a peripheral society.

The concepts of *industrial* and/or *class society* ... revolved around the issue of how socially produced wealth could be distributed in a socially unequal and also *legitimate* way. (Beck, U., 1992, p. 19)

The concepts of the transitional post-communist society revolve around the issue of how politically produced negative effects, risks and peripheral states of mind and living could be re-distributed at the expense of those who are not part of a game governed by 'privilege-generative mechanisms' (Voinea, C. F., 2017). In this way, welfare-state protections and regulations become a tool used not to help those disfavoured people but to redistribute the effects (uncompensated) of a transposed communist 'elite lifestyle'.[2] The

---

2   The discussion around an elite lifestyle in Central and Eastern Europe appears to divide in two historical periods: communist, circumscribing historical developments during post-war Central and Eastern Europe (1945-1989) and post- communist period, starting with 1989. 'In post-war Eastern Europe, it was soon widely recognised that membership of the communist party didn't just give you political standing, but also provided access to numerous socio-economic advantages. Possession of a party card opened the door to numerous "perks", including the allocation of superior standard of accommodation, access to special shops (containing domestically produced goods in short supply and imported luxury items from the West) and holidays in special health resorts.' (Hignet,

newly emerged post-communist 'managerialism' inherited characteristics of the former communist elites.

The new power elite of post-communism is not composed of owners, but rather of the technocratic-managerial elite together with the new 'politocracy which constitute its dominant fraction, and elite humanistic and social science intellectuals which form its dominated fraction. (Szelenyi, I et al., 1997)

The distinctiveness of the new welfare capitalism in Central and Eastern Europe bears the imprint of a 'coalition of class fractions and elites' (Ibid) which is different from a 'capitalist class whose ability to garner profits and to exploit workers is rooted in private ownership of the means of production, that is, economic capital' (Ibid). The capitalistic spirit in the Western societies is rooted in a rationalised capitalist mode of reproduction whereas the 'combination of production and consumption' (Higgins, E., 2015) in the Eastern European societies is governed by a coalition between a 'technocratic-managerial elite' and a 'new politocracy' whose main expectations become drivers of a new risk society.

The new approach to the existing political capitalism theory in Central and Eastern Europe could be described by referring to a peripheral 'system dependency syndrome' (Badescu & Badescu, 2014), a system maintained by new coalitions and their modelling power. We identified a new type of 'self- fulfilling prophecy', a concept originated by Robert K. Merton (1948). Elites in the West, as well as in Eastern Europe, have a common denominator: their self-fulfilling states. Such states point to the modelling power of the system that causes individuals as well as entities' expectations to become a new lifestyle.

> The big corporations accumulated not only a great amount of wealth but, also, an extraordinary power of modelling lifestyles at a global scale (Badescu & Badescu, 2014, p. 18)

The 'paradigm of risk society' gains significance based on the solution

---

K. (2012). Source: https:// thevieweast.wordpress.com/2012/04/23/power-and-privilege-in-communist-eastern-europe/ (accessed 05.08.2019))

of a different problem: 'how can risks and hazards systematically produced as part of modernization be prevented, minimized, dramatized or channelized?' (Beck, U., 1992, p. 19)

> How can they be limited and distributed away so that they neither hamper the modernization process nor exceed the limits of that which is tolerable— ecologically, psychologically and socially? (Ibid)

As a matter of fact, the post-communist society is confronted with two different series of problems: of how to release itself from political constraints and how to cope with the new political constraints and risks of living in a peripheral society which undertakes destructive processes. We are no longer exclusively concerned with releasing mankind from traditional constraint or even with releasing people from the risks of reflexive modernization, but, foremost, with the risks emerged from a political elite which believes itself as making new social arrangements, while it is in fact a rent-seeker.

Rent-seeking becomes the epitome of a society whose circulation of elites is induced by a pseudo-legitimacy deeply rooted in:

> State capture (firms shaping and affecting formulation of the rules of the game through private payments to public officials and politicians) with influence (doing the same without recourse to payments) and with administrative corruption ('petty' forms of bribery in connection with the implementation of laws, rules, and regulations). (Hellman, J. S. et al., 2000)

Elite becomes a pseudo-elite, a surviving elite whose power, authority and legitimacy are given by their ability of rent-appropriation. The bargaining power of the ruling class in a society where various actors are involved to a certain extent in the process of rent appropriation confers its imprint. We may call this process 'de-reflexive post-modernization.'

We therefore need not only a paradigm of risk society (cf. Beck, U., 1992), but a paradigm of risks that accompanies 'de-reflexive post- modernization'. Beck drew our attention to what he called 'reflexive modernization':

We are therefore concerned [...] with problems resulting from techno-economic development itself. *Modernization is becoming reflexive; it is becoming its own theme.* Questions of the development and employment of technologies (in the realm of nature, society, and personality) are being eclipsed by questions of the political and economic management of the risks of actually or potentially utilized technologies – discovering, administering, acknowledging such hazards with respect to specially.

The distribution of socially produced wealth and related conflicts occupy the foreground so long as obvious material need, the 'dictatorship of scarcity, rules the thought and action of people (as today in large part of the so-called 'Third World'). Under these conditions of 'scarcity society,' the modernization process takes place with the claim of opening the gates to hidden sources of social wealth with the keys of techno-scientific development. (Beck, U., 1992, p. 20)

In western societies, 'the struggle for one's 'daily bread' has lost its urgency' (Ibid). On the other hand, more and more destructive forces are being unleashed via the modernization process. The social positions and conflicts of a 'wealth distributing' society begin to be joined by those of a 'risk-distributing society.' In West Germany, the beginning of this transition can be located to the early 1970s. Two types of topics and conflicts overlap here. There are two societies in one: 'scarcity society' and 'risk distributing society.'

What thus emerges in risk society is the political potential of catastrophes ... Managing these can include a reorganization of power and authority. Risk society is a catastrophic society. In it the exceptional condition threatens to become the norm. (Ibid, p. 24)

A new type of enquiry somehow related to the idea that 'power, democracy or welfare are relationally structured phenomena' (Ibid, p. 26) is required within a new typology of the welfare regimes.

Regime type in the Central and Eastern Europe: Insecurity or informality?

THE PROCESS OF DE-REFLEXIVE POST-MODERNIZATION REFERS TO THE diminishing of systemic reflexivity of the modern capitalism as resulting from those phenomena and processes that induce volatile states, inflation, diminishing of the control capability on sides effects of globalization and expansion of the system itself etc. Western society increased its capability of controlling sides effects of capitalism expansion by developing gradually that type of welfare system highly codified based on the evolutionary logic of the Western capitalism. Esping-Andersen's three Western types of the welfare capitalism (1990) are an illustration of its systemic reflexivity.

Our working hypothesis is that 'de-reflexivity of post-modernization' in Eastern European societies results in the prevalence of what Sharks and Gough (2010) used to call the *'insecurity regimes' of welfare*. A welfare regime or another reflects the interaction between the family, the state and the market, showing how broad and deep the effects of de-reflexive postmodernity appear to be, and of political elite behaviour in the Eastern societies during so-called 'transition' period.

Towards a New Type of Welfare State in Central and Eastern Europe

THE TRANSITION PROCESS IN COUNTRIES FROM CENTRAL AND EASTERN Europe has to deal with its own path-dependent dynamic when searching for those appropriate options of welfare policy. Our findings revealed differences between the Central and Eastern European welfare regime and the Western type. What are the causes of such differences?

There is a long debate on the dynamics of transition process in Central and Eastern European countries. The complexity of the transition process might be derived from the particularities of a certain type of economic, social as well as institutional arrangements. We are more concerned with providing an explanation of the dynamics of such arrangements in different countries from Central and Eastern Europe. We believe there is a 'potential for a lock-in' when trying to depict the dynamics of transition process in post-communist societies. Kominek refers to 'a lock-in [...] comparable to the situation of an institution which changes only incrementally at the most (North, 1990)' (Kominek, 2009, p. 3). The transition process refers, also, to those institutional changes so that such situation is similar to saying that the transition takes place within a 'self-reinforcing process with the potential for a lock-in' (Sydow et al., 2005) This potential for lock-in might be caused by those specific economic, social as well as institutional arrangements. This 'lock-in' factor raises the issue of regime type in the comparative literature on welfare regimes. The path dependency theory provides a perspective on the nature of transition process. A transition, from a macro-perspective, is a transformation process when actors act upon their social, economic and institutional arrangements in a self-reinforcing process.

Our hypothesis is that the political elite in the Central and Eastern European (CEE) societies are de-reflexive elites, so that their potential for the self-reinforcing strategies is reduced. De-reflexive elites act through a self- less-reinforcing process.

Maclean, M. et al. refers to elites exhibiting:

> Five' types of reflexive behaviour, from which two modes of reflexive practice were derived: an *accumulative* mode, through which business leaders reflexively accumulate capital, positions and perspectives; and a *re-constructive* mode, through which they re-constitute the self in response to contingences, contexts and insights gathered.'
> (Maclean, M. et al., 2012)

Elites in the CEE nations exhibit a *self-centred accumulative mode*, meaning that they accumulate for creating their own luxurious lifestyle through a *de-reflexive augmentation* of 'capital, positions and perspectives'. Moreover, such a de-reflexive behaviour induces a de-constructive mode 'through which they re-constitute', this time, their *self- centred, egoistic conduct* 'in response to contingences, contexts and insights gathered' (Ibid) in the process of capitalist reproduction.

Ultimately, this type of elite will proceed to a minimal mobilization to acting upon the social, economic and institutional arrangements that would stimulate a self-reinforcing process. Instead of such a mobilization, the political elite opts for oligarchical arrangements, that is, for pursuing their own interest instead of pursuing the social interest. An 'insecurity welfare regime' emerges from such a self-centred accumulative behaviour. A deficit of collective motivation is one main characteristic of a *de-reflexive elite*. It is the main cause of *lock-in potential,* that is, of a decreasing 'self-reinforcing' capability needed to face the challenges of transition period within the Central and Eastern European societies. The comparative datasets unveil such a phenomenon through the so-called index of welfare loss. The index is reflected in the paradox of inflation which makes intelligible the process through which capitalization embeds a hidden loss. Friedman considers such a phenomenon one that accompanies the process of money circulation. The problem is that such a paradoxical effect is approached differently in the Western societies compared to the East. Such an effect, called the 'paradox of inflation', is redistributed in the unilateral disadvantage of low and low-middle class in Eastern societies. Such a redistributive process leads to the differentiation of Western-type welfare regimes from Eastern-type and it seems to be owed to the de-reflexive profile of political elite within Eastern part of Europe.

Let us comprehend the phenomenon. I shall invoke Giddens' theoretical perspective that has contributed to the development of the path dependence theory by means of his concept as well as theoretical construct of the 'duality of structure':

> According to the notion of the duality of structure, the structural properties of social systems are both medium and outcome of the practices they recursively organize. Structure is not 'external' to individuals: as memory traces, and as instantiated in social practices, it is in a certain sense more 'internal' than exterior to their activities [...]. (Giddens, 1984, p. 25)

It is the self-reinforcing process that shed light on the dynamics of transition regarded as a process of institutional design in post-communist societies. The actors involved in designing the new institutions act upon the new institutional arrangements and the new medium created within these new institutions act upon their originators:

> Thus, structure is the result of e.g. an institutionalization and also functions as a medium. Applied in this description of an institutionalization, the beginning existence of an institution is a result of the actor's behaviour. But as a medium it also effects the actor's next decisions and actions and thus again influences the process of institutionalization. (Kominek, J., p. 23)

The concept of 'duality of structure' might be as well applied to economic systems and within this new perspective we should pinpoint the real-nominal duality in economics. Scientists have to take into account the influence of inflation in compiling various social and economic indicators. The question is whether inflation is the only influencing factor when depicting this duality between nominal and real value, between what we would consider as being the given or the induced perceived value of something and that super added perception of a monetarist phenomenon like inflation. *The only difference is that, within this new perspective of duality what is added is subtracted from what we believe as being given.* The inflation is a monetary phenomenon (cf. Friedman, 1970) and each time money changes hands, the inflation is making a dent in the value so that the real value is diminished with the loss due to inflation. The debate about the cause and effects of inflation falls outside the scope of this chapter. Nevertheless, the structural properties of economic systems explained from the perspective of duality of structure raise the issue of considering the phenomenon of inflation as a medium and as an outcome because it recursively organizes the way in which a loss in value due to inflation is considered a super added element and subtracted from the nominal value of the money. *The inflation has gained its dual significance as a phenomenon capable of being a medium as it is embedded in the value of the money and, consequently, being the outcome as the inflation becomes evident through its perceptible indication, that is, the real value of something.*

We believe the phenomenon of inflation can generate its own 'self' through a self-reinforcing process in which actors are reinforced to keep up the process. Inflation generates, therefore, a hidden self, a perverse self who acts upon most social and economic processes. Therefore, it is requested to underline that in any type of society, two factors act upon the welfare regimes: de-reflexive elites and inflationary self. The second is owed to the system itself (the world capitalism), the other is owed to Eastern-type political systems. Both are responsible for the profile of welfare regimes which, because of these two factors, generate *defective regimes* as in the East or *effective regimes* as in the Western part of the world. The actors, either the individuals or institutions, are agents involved, virtually, everywhere, in monetary transactions. Formula of duality of structure in economics is as follows:

> GIVEN or ASSIGNED ELEMENT [Nominal value (induced perceived value)] + SUPER ADDED ELEMENT [Inflation regarded as a phenomenon leading to a loss of value] = REAL VALUE

The difference between nominal value and real value of the money is an indicator of reflexivity of the capitalist system itself. Anticipating the subsequent explanations in the present chapter, we shall point out that the difference between the nominal and implicit VAT rate is an indicator of the reflexivity of political system and of the elite within a given country or group of countries within a regional world. These two indicators can be used to evaluate the systemic reflexivity within a certain society and to measure the disparity between the welfare regimes within different countries and regional worlds. Based on these indicators we may calculate the index of welfare loss and, consequently, of the political and fiscal de-reflexivity within a certain society.

Political and Fiscal De-reflexivity

TWO FACTORS ACT UPON THE WELFARE REGIMES IN EASTERN EUROPE: *de-reflexive elites* and *inflationary self*. The second one is owed to the capitalist system itself, the other is owed to *Eastern political system*. I shall underline also that in a society where the de-reflexive elites prevail, we also have a defective redistributive system. The consequences of de-reflexive redistributive system become evident when referring to the amplitude of what is called tax evasion phenomenon. The difference between nominal and implicit VAT rates is due to the reflexivity of the system not to a presumed inclination towards criminal behaviours of economic actors. Such a difference can be described using a set of fiscal indicators like *nominal tax rate* and *implicit tax rate,* the last one reflecting the real measure of *fiscal impact.* The impact of inflation on various social and economic indicators will be analysed in the following section. Our first task is to find out what are the most important taxes from the perspective of their revenue contribution to the general consolidated budget. V.A.T. and social contributions generated, altogether, almost 48% of tax revenue according to the execution of the general consolidated budget in Romania in 2017. V.A.T. has become an 'essential source of revenue in more than 150 countries' according to a review of global indirect tax developments issued by Ernst & Young in 2013. Our next task is to comparatively evaluate the difference between the nominal rates (of VAT and insurance contributions) and their implicit rates, depicting the real picture of the redistributive process in the selected Central and Eastern European countries. It is the difference between the *legal tax rate* and *implicit tax rate* that reveals the de-reflexive profile of redistributive system and of political elite in this part of the world. Comparing differences between nominal and implicit rates in 2012 versus 2010 (see Table 3) reveals an increasing trend in the cases of Romania, Lithuania, Hungary, Poland and Slovakia, although this trend was reversed in the following period (2013-2015, see Table 4), partly due to a cut of VAT rates.

Differences between nominal rate and implicit rate of social contributions in the selected time intervals (2010-2012 and 2013-2015) were among the highest in Romania comparing with the rest of CEE countries included in our comparative analysis (see Tables 5 and 6). Higher the differences between nominal rates and implicit rates, lower the reflexivity potential of societies, indicating a de-reflexive tendency. Comparing social contribution rates along with differences between nominal and implicit rates between Romania and the rest of CEE countries confirms our de-

TABLE 3. VAT rates and the differences between V.A.T. rate and the implicit V.A.T. rate in countries from CEE (2010-2012)

Countries	VAT rates			Implicit V.A.T. rates[1]			Differences between V.A.T. rate and implicit V.A.T. rate		
	2010	2011	2012	2010	2011	2012	2010	2011	2012
BG	20.0	20.0	20.0	14.4	13.8	14.2	5.6	6.2	5.8
CZ	20.0	20.0	20.0	13.5	13.7	14.2	6.5	6.3	5.8
EE	20.0	20.0	20.0	16.5	16.4	16.9	3.5	3.6	3.1
LV	21.0	22.0	21.5	10.3	10.8	11.3	10.7	11.2	10.2
LT	21.0	21.0	21.0	12.2	12.3	11.8	8.8	8.7	9.2
HU	25.0	25.0	27.0	16.3	15.9	17.0	8.7	9.1	10
PL	22.0	23.0	23.0	12.4	12.9	11.7	9.6	10.1	11.3
RO	21.5	24.0	24.0	12.0	13.8	13.7	9.5	10.2	10.3
SI	20.0	20.0	20.0	14.7	14.3	14.3	5.3	5.7	5.7
SK	19.0	20.0	20.0	10.7	11.7	10.4	8.3	8.3	9.6

Source: European Commission, EUROSTAT, Ministry of Finance, Fiscal Council, own compilation

TABLE 4. VAT rates and the differences between V.A.T. rate and the implicit V.A.T. rate in countries from CEE (2013 – 2015)

Countries	VAT rates			Implicit V.A.T. rates[1]			Differences between V.A.T. rate and implicit V.A.T. rate		
	2013	2014	2015	2013	2014	2015	2013	2014	2015
BG	17.2	17.2	17.1	14.9	14.2	14.7	2.3	3	2.4
CZ	18.9	18.9	18.8	15.0	15.4	15.6	3.9	3.5	3.2
EE	18.9	18.8	18.8	16.0	16.8	17.6	2.9	2.0	1.2
LV	19.5	19.4	19.4	12.1	12.4	12.5	7.4	7	6.9
LT	19.4	19.3	19.3	11.9	12.1	12.1	7.5	7.2	7.2
HU	22.9	21.8	21.7	17.1	18.6	19.8	5.8	3.2	1.9
PL	16.9	16.8	17.1	11.6	11.9	12.0	5.3	4.9	5.1
RO	21.5	20.8	18.4	13.5	12.7	13.3	8.0	8.1	5.1
SI	15.4	16.4	16.5	15.4	15.9	16.1	-	0.5	0.4
SK	18.7	18.9	18.7	11.2	11.7	12.4	7.5	7.2	6.3

Source: European Commission, EUROSTAT, Ministry of Finance, Fiscal Council, own compilation

reflexive hypothesis. In 2012, for instance, social contributions rate in Romania was amongst the highest in the region (44.4%) and the difference between nominal and implicit rates in the same case was the highest (15.8) whereas, for instance, in the case of Czech Republic the nominal rate was the highest (45.3%) and the difference between the nominal rate and the real rate was negative (see Table 5). A reflexive hypothesis is confirmed in the case of Czech Republic where a negative figure depicts an efficient taxation system.

Table 5. Social contributions rates (SCRs) and the differences between SCRs and implicit rates in countries from CEE (2010-2012)

Countries	Social contributions rate (SCR)[1]			Social contributions implicit rate (SCIR)[2]			Differences between SCR and SCIR		
	2010	2011	2012	2010	2011	2012	2010	2011	2012
BG	28.9	31.0	31.0	21.3	22.6	22.8	7.6	8.4	8.2
CZ	45.3	45.3	45.3	47.7	47.8	47.8	-2.4	-2.5	-2.5
EE	37.2	37.2	37.2	36.5	35.2	33.4	0.7	2	3.8
LV	33.1	35.1	35.1	23.4	25.0	24.7	9.7	10.1	10.4
LT	40.1	40.1	40.1	36.5	36.2	35.9	3.6	3.9	4.2
HU	44.0	44.5	47.0	33.1	36.6	35.7	10.9	8.3	11.3
PL	37.9	37.6	39.6	34.5	36.5	NA	3.4	1.6	NA
RO	44.4	44.4	44.4	29.2	30.1	28.6	15.2	14.3	15.8
SI	38.2	38.2	38.2	33.1	33.4	33.8	5.1	4.8	4.4
SK	48.6	48.6	48.6	42.2	42.4	43.5	6.4	6.2	5.1

Source: European Commission, EUROSTAT, Ministry of Finance, Fiscal Council, own compilation

Table 6. Social contributions rates (SCRs) and the differences between SCRs and implicit rates in countries from CEE (2013-2015)

Countries	Social contributions (rate (SCR)[1]			Social contributions implicit rate (SCIR)[2]			Differences between SCR and SCIR		
	2013	2014	2015	2013	2014	2015	2013	2014	2015
BG	31.0	31.0	31.0	22.0	22.5	23.2	9	8.5	7.8
CZ	45.3	45.3	45.3	47.7	48.4	49.1	-2.4	-3.1	-3.8
EE	37.2	36.0	35.4	32.9	32.4	31.9	4.3	3.6	3.5
LV	35.1	35.1	34.1	25.7	24.6	23.3	10.6	10.5	10.8
LT	40.1	40.1	40.0	35.9	36.6	37.2	4.2	3.5	2.8
HU	47.0	47.0	47.0	38.0	38.9	39.0	9	8.1	8
PL	39.6	39.6	39.4	42.5	42.2	NA	2.9	2.6	NA
RO	44.4	43.1	39.4	33.2	31.9	29.9	11.2	11.2	9.5
SI	38.2	38.2	38.2	34.7	34.6	35.4	3.5	3.6	2.8
SK	48.6	48.6	48.6	47.0	46.9	47.5	1.6	1.7	1.1

Source: European Commission, EUROSTAT, Ministry of Finance, Fiscal Council, own compilation

Figures of social contribution rates, both nominal and implicit (see Tables 5-6) indicate a divergent evolution among selected countries: Romania has not only the highest social contribution rates but a high dis-incentivizing fiscal system due to a de-reflexive redistribution system, signalling significant social risks. These are all facts that contributed to the generation of a new type of welfare system in Central and Eastern European countries. A welfare system is based on redistributive processes but, in this case, such redistributions give the area. The main idea is that such new disequilibrium may be explained through a deviation process that become part of what we might consider as a new welfare regime in Central and Eastern Europe. Part of the redistributive process within the newly formed welfare system is deviated nuances to characters of a fiscal disincentive. The evidence of such de-reflexive welfare systems arises from the differences between nominal and implicit tax rates. We believe the action of *a de-reflexive elite* in this part of the world induces a structural disequilibrium of the welfare system owed to a low power of reflexivity in terms of political legitimacy and fiscal disincentive in from its normal functioning due to the influences of this so-called *de-reflexive elite*. There is a new type of redistributive process leading to such significant differences between nominal and implicit taxation rates like VAT and social contributions as shown in the tables above (No. 3 to 6). These differences can spot elements of *defective regimes* in Central and Eastern Europe.

IN THE QUEST OF WELFARE: SOCIAL CORRIDORS OF MIGRATION AND THE REMITTANCES FROM WELFARE REGIMES TO REGIMES OF WELFARE CORRIDORS

Towards a typology of trans-boundary welfare regimes in the CEE

GLOBALIZATION IS A FRAMING PROCESS OF CAPITALIST WORLD EXTENSION. This process occurs through continuous remaking of social spatiality defined by the boundaries of welfare regimes, i.e., through contradictory ongoing process of commodification and de-commodification. The commodification process tends to transform anything into a privatized form of commodity essential for the reproduction of capitalism. On the contrary, the de-commodification process tends to use anything in the service of the family members of the workers. The globalizing process reveals, on the other hand, to be an unexpected opportunity for the labour factor (employment), that is, for workers, to optimize their own social condition by expanding the boundaries of welfare regimes. The boundaries of welfare regimes stem from invoking spatiality within two identifiable contexts: spatiality of 'ongoing processes of commodification' (Prodnik, J, 2012, p. 1) and spatiality of ongoing processes of de-commodification.

Processes of transforming literally anything into a

> privatized form of (fictitious) commodity that is exchanged
> in the circulation process are of fundamental importance
> for the rise and reproduction of capitalism. (Ibid)

'At the same time commodity, as the "cell-form of capitalism"' (Ibid) allows encountering the singularity of aspatial dimension of reproduction of capitalism. On the other hand, the reproduction of capitalism gets through a process of de-commodification imposed by the need for distributing and redistributing goods, not only for those who possess the capital and labour, but also for those who are the members of their own families.

My proposal is to rethink the welfare state theory/hypothesis by considering the effect that the social corridors of remittances ('cross border network') wield upon the welfare regimes within a given area. The process itself goes through social space reconstruction and social corridors of migration are the places where the new social space emerges. Technically, the variable that measures the effect of 'cross-border network' (entailed by migration) on the welfare regime is the value (amount) of remittances. The reproduction of capitalism experiences such a contending process.

Welfare policies are not successful in securing sustainable employment within the national borders: 'Ninety million people migrate for work globally every year' (BSR, 2008, p. 1). Social corridors of international migration emerged because of this decision. The phenomenon of social corridors is the symptom of the emergence of a new vector, hence a non-equipollence between capital, employment and taxation.

Having access to the syntagma of structural power (i.e. the capability to manage the structures of network power) helped me to conceptualize this new vector/power that emerged at the intersection of the three factors (capital, employment and taxation) in the new international migration context. New ways of spatializing the relationships between these three factors emerge along with the classical spatialization that is usually called national space. The space emerged in the wake of the new vectors of international migration takes the shape of social corridors of migration, whereas the space emerged in the wake of capital flows takes the shape of supra-national organizational settings.

Remittance corridors become strong descriptors of what appears as the new geography of welfare. A new type and a new conception of redistributive systems emerge. It is embedded into a trans-boundary redistributive pattern that overlaps the transnational corridors of migration.

It has become evident that the welfare states from the CEE possess limited capabilities to provide the social safety net. The remittance corridors compensate for this limited capability. The flows of remittances from migrant workers to their families in their home countries show a new type of redistribution that stretches out across national borders, depicting a new variable of welfare state regimes, namely *regimes of welfare corridors*.

Cases of welfare corridors

REMITTANCE CORRIDORS BECOME STRONG PREDICTORS OF THE TRANS-boundary redistributive patterns. Income is redistributed among groups of a population spread across large geographic areas, continents and even at a global scale. 'Social well-being' is distributed not only among groups of a population of a state, but also within larger geographic areas spanning across states, regions, continents and even the entire world. We need a new conception and method for depicting the new constructivist perspective on redistributing general well-being. The new concept is the *case of welfare corridors*, which should encompass the trans-boundary redistributive patterns along the remittance corridors. This concept covers a scaling process, a new social technic used to correct the structural asymmetry of postmodern capitalism. A case of welfare corridors also facilitates an unexpected outcome in terms of spotting local comparative disproportion of incomes among different ethnic segments of labour. The next two sections elaborate two cases of migratory patterns located in two different geographic areas. The first section is focused on identifying patterns of migration based on the bilateral estimations of migration stocks and remittances in the case of Romania and Poland. The second section identifies drivers of migration in Sub-Saharan Africa. Two dominant cases of welfare corridors were identified when comparing the Romanian migration patterns with Polish ones: the *Mediterranean case* (Italy and Spain) as prevailing over the *Nordic case* (Austria, Germany, U.K., France, Belgium, Sweden, Ireland, Netherlands). Migration to countries belonging to the North-Western case barely amounted to 8% of the total, in the case of Romania, while the Mediterranean corridor appears to be dominant (52.4%).

In *Poland's case*, the *Nordic corridor* (both North-Western Central European area and North-Western area) (Austria, Germany, Hungary, U.K., France, Belgium, Sweden, Ireland, Netherlands) appeared to be dominant (61.5%) while the Mediterranean corridor plays a secondary role (5%).

Another dimension of our comparative synopsis regards the disproportion of incomes when comparing ethnic origins of migrant stocks. For instance, Polish migrants could produce higher incomes (1353

Table 7. Groups of destination countries, bilateral estimations of migration stocks and remittances in the case of Romania and Poland (2017)

Corridors of remittances	Romania				Poland			
	Bilateral estimation of migration stocks in 2017	% total remittances	Remittances (millions USD) e2017	Remittances per migrant (USD)	Bilateral estimation of migration stocks in 2017	% total remittances	Remittances (millions USD) e2017	Remittances per migrant (USD)
North-Western and Central European corridor (Austria, Germany, Hungary)	840,749	21.8	1076	1280	1,409,624	32.9	2236	1586
Mediteranean corridor (Italy, Spain)	1.663,808	52.4	2591	1557	167,119	5.1	347	2076
Transatlantic corridor (USA, Canada)	257,660	8.5	423	1641	620,640	18.2	1236	1992
North-Western corridor (U.K., France, Belgium, Sweden, Ireland, Netherlands)	569,721	7.9	392	688	1,436,853	28,6	1944	1353
Southern corridor (Israel)	77,770	3.1	151	1942	57,824	1.5	104	1799
Total	3,409,708	93.7	4633		3,692,060	86.2	5876	

Sources: Bilateral Remittance Estimates for 2017, The World Bank; Bilateral Estimates of Migrant Stocks in 2017, The World Bank; own compilation

USD remittances per migrant) when looking at North-Western case (U.K., France, Belgium, Sweden, Ireland, Netherlands) compared with the Romanians (688 USD remittances per migrant). Such a high disproportion could indicate differentiated access to jobs. A comparative perspective (2017 versus 2010) (see Tables 8 and 9) on the average value of remittances per migrant, as well as on the bilateral estimation of migration stocks, reveals a significant change of migration preferences in both cases: migration stocks more than doubled in the cases of Romanians and Polish living in countries belonging to the North-Western Central European corridor (Austria, Germany, Hungary) followed by a steep decline in the average value of remittances per Polish migrant (35% less of its comparative value) as compared to a Romanian who sent back, on average, 10% less than in 2010.

It is also worth noting that the Romanian migrant population stocks in countries belonging to the North-Western corridor more than tripled in 2017 compared to 2010, although the average value of remittances per migrant halved for the same period.

Table 8. Groups of destination countries, bilateral estimations of migration stocks and remittances in the case of Romania and Poland (2010)

Corridors of remittances	Romania				Poland			
	Bilateral estimatiion of migration stocks in 2010	% total remittances	Remittances (millions USD) 2010	Remittances per migrant (USD)	Bilateral estimatiion of migration stocks in 2010	% total remittances	Remittances (millions USD) 2010	Remittances per migrant (USD)
North-Western Central European corridor (Austria, Germany, Hungary)	380.898	13.6	537	1410	690.232	22.24	1685	2441
Mediteranean corridor (Italy, Spain)	1.623.508	58.6	2315	1426	204.280	6.4	485	2374
Transatlantic corridor (USA, Canada)	267.461	10.12	400	1496	686.410	22.4	1697	2472
North-Western corridor (U.K.,France, Belgium, Sweden, Ireland, Netherland)	166.602	6.12	242	1453	883.900	28.12	2130	2410
Southern corridor (Israel)	182.099	6.12	253	1389	117.287	3.6	272	2319
Total	2.769.053				3.155.509			

Sources: Bilateral Remittance for 2010, The World Bank; Bilateral Estimates of Migrant Stocks in 2010, The World Bank, own compilation

The case of Ethiopia – South Africa 'migration corridor'

A NEW WAVE OF CHANGE IN TERMS OF NEW CONCEPTUALIZATIONS WAS triggered by the study of migration in the age of globalization (Chetail, V., Zapata, 2013; Nyberg-Sorensen, N. et al., 2003; Louis, M., 2013) with either migrants being key drivers (de Haas, 2010; Faist, 2008; Kunz, 2008) or forces 'which get migration going and keep it going once begun' (Van Hear, N et al., 2012). The study of globalization has also brought about an expanded debate in terms of institutional involvement with international organizations such as the World Bank and the IMF increasingly involved in the new debate, circumscribing the problematic of migration-development nexus (Kunz, 2008; Ratha and Shaw, 2007). The current discussion on the drivers of migration has fed into recent initiatives such as the 'Global Commission on Migration and Development (2003-5), the UN High-Level Dialogue on Migration and Development (2006) and the ongoing Global Forum on Migration and Development' (Van Hear, N et al. 2012).

Debates surrounding issues of globalization and inequality have also gained traction (Goldin and Reinert, 2006; Held and Kaya, 2007). Globalization has become a mitigating factor in terms of poverty alleviation (Held and Kaya, 2007) although there are voices arguing that the process of globalization has also increased inequality (Wade, 2004; Maskin, 2014).

There are studies (cf. Bastia, 2013) arguing that the literature is centred on countries of the North, 'continuing to be couched in binary assumptions' (Ibid). The discussion needs to go beyond the well-known 'narrowly economistic point of view' (Ibid). There is on-going debate on what we may call 'kinetics' of migration: 'there are forces which lead to the

Table 9. Global Migrant Stocks (millions)

Migrants in ⟍ Migrants from	Developing countries	High-income OECD countries	High-income non-OECD countries	Total
Developing countries	73.9	61.8	20.1	**155.8**
High-income OECD countries	3.4	25.5	1.2	**30.1**
High-income non-OECD countries	0.8	3.6	0.3	**4.7**
Total	**78**	**90.9**	**21.6**	**191**

Source: University of Sussex and World Bank data based on UN (2005), individual censuses, OECD (2006), and others.

inception of migration and to the perpetuation of movement' (Van Hear, N. et al., 2012). Such forces can be identified as 'key drivers of migration' (Ibid). The debate is still open to the investigation of a *translative migration*. Ethiopia, for instance, experiences a special dynamic of migration which has its roots in rural areas where the population is poorer and in search for a better life in urban regions either in Ethiopia or abroad. In this case, the inception of migration is identified in rural areas while the perpetuation of movement is translated into urban areas. The translative process has its own causation. The Ethiopian rural population is too poor to afford to migrate abroad. Therefore, there is an initial migratory phase when the migration takes place internally between rural and urban areas.

The extent of an uneven South-South migration

THE WORLD BANK (2007) IDENTIFIED SEVERAL ESTIMATES OF SOUTH-South migration. One suggests that South-South migration 'may account for 47% (74 million) of all migration from the South' (World Bank, 2007) (See Table 10). UNPD also indicates that 'half of the migrants from developing countries migrate to other developing countries' (Ibid). South-South migration is uneven across regions and even continents. Nevertheless, there are three regions that have come to the fore: Europe and Central Asia; Sub-Saharan Africa (SSA) and South Asia. (cf. Connor, P., 2018) The unprecedented dynamic of migration in SSA signals an imperative for theoretical and empirical debate around key drivers of migration.

Many migrants in SSA are low-skilled, facing barriers to mobility. 'Such individuals could have insufficient human capital to command high wages' (Uprety, D., Sylwester, K., 2017). In the case of Ethiopia, such inability is reflected in the value of the average remittances that is relatively low compared with total expenditure of the household with remittances (FAO United Nations). An Ethiopian household can have annual total expenditures without remittances around $3500 comparing with slightly more than $4000 if remittances are included (Ibid).

Moreover, remittances are not invested (Hassan, S. and Negash, M., 2013) in 'income-generating activities' (Bakewell, 2011) Considering

South Africa as not only destination country but, also, as origin country of migration, Pendleton argues (cf. Ibid) that remittances in this country may not have 'developmental value', a situation that could be replicated in the case of Ethiopia. Therefore, the income generated by migrants does not create a solid basis for a better quality of life, especially in rural areas.

Driving out of poverty?

THE INVESTIGATION OF SOCIO-ECONOMIC DRIVERS OF MIGRATION IN Ethiopia (cf. FAO United Nations) reveals a distinct pattern compared to other African countries. The economic drivers are prevalent in rural areas comparing with family factors which are dominant in the case of urban area. It reflects a 'discrepancy of decent employment opportunities between urban and rural areas in many developing countries' (Ibid). Comparing rural with urban areas of Ethiopian migration reveals not only a discrepancy in terms of employment opportunities but, also a 'limited access to social protection' (Ibid). The discussion now turns to summarizing several drivers of migration.

Socio-economic driver

THE INVESTIGATION OF INTERNAL AND INTERNATIONAL ETHIOPIAN migration reveals a highly gendered dimension. Family is the most common reason for internal and international migration in the case of Ethiopia (Ibid): Women are more likely to migrate for family reasons, predominantly from rural areas in the case of internal migration (Ibid). The internal migration is more frequent than international migration (cf. Ibid).

Ethiopian migration to other African countries is economically motivated (Kuschminder, K et al., 2012) although the same study signalled that 'females also dominate migration within Africa at 53%, which appears contrary to the common perception in Ethiopia that migration to African countries is male-dominated' (Ibid). Family reunification, along with other drivers, like security reasons and education opportunities, are responsible for migration to the north and other African countries (Ibid). A structural analysis of Ethiopian migrants will reveal the socio-economic profile of Ethiopian migration to South-Africa. For instance, there is a high variation of migration's gender dimension when considering Ethiopian migration within Sub-Saharan Africa. Profiling Ethiopian migration to other African countries (Ibid) reveals that 'the majority of migrants to South Africa are male, at 82%, and the majority of migrants to Sudan are female, at 75%' (Ibid).

The classical literature on migration drivers is mainly anchored in so-called 'push-pull' models. My intention is to expand such a 'push-pull' framework by incorporating a different complex or configuration which shapes migration corridors. The reason for such an expanded perspective is that 'migration drivers work in combination – in what can be termed driver complexes – to shape the specific form and structure of population movements' (Van Hear, N. et al., 2012).

The Ethiopian case reveals the interconnected relationships between socio-economic factors, gender and migration patterns. The gender dimension is emphasized within the interconnectedness of migration drivers. It may be useful to investigate the dynamics of the migration process by 'distinguishing between predisposing, proximate, precipitating and mediating factors' (Ibid).

Predisposing factors create the context for generating migration. Scanning the macro-political as well as the macro-economic environments could reveal the 'context in which migration is more likely'. 79% of the total Ethiopian population is projected to live in rural areas by the end of 2019 (Central Statistical Agency) and depend on subsistence farming (Hassan, S. and Negash, M., 2013). There is a land shortage which induces a push factor of migration from rural to urban area. Migration in Ethiopia is dynamic in terms of its translation from an internal migration rooted in rural area to an urban driven international migration. Perpetuation of movement between rural and urban areas could reveal 'structural disparities between places of migrant origin and destination shaped by the macro-political economy'

(Van Hear, N. et al., 2012).

Proximate factors include changes in macro-political environment that could have more bearing on migration, favouring the perpetuation of movement, for instance, from urban Ethiopian area to other urban areas in South-Africa. Hassan, S. and Negash, M. identified 'abject poverty and bad governance' as dominant push factors while 'demand-pull factors, represented by better economic opportunities and jobs in the host (new) country' (Hassan, S. and Negash, M., 2013) facilitate the perpetuation of movement across-borders. Push factors could disfavour the perpetuation of movement internally by 'prohibiting citizens from freely moving within regions, hence denying them the basic constitutional right of mobility' (Ibid). There are cases when prohibiting citizens to move freely bears the imprint of extreme measures. For instance, 'the expulsion of 'others' from the Benishangul-Gumuz, Gura Ferda and the Ogaden regions, considered by many to be crime against humanity' (Ibid) is the extreme version of a rather distortionary macro-environment which enables the transformation of proximate factors into a *precipitating factor*. 'Precipitating factors are those that actually trigger departure.' (Van Hear, N et al. 2012) Other factors like the drought and climate change 'exacerbate both the despair and the outmigration' (Hassan, S. and Negash, M. 2013). The country has not been self-sufficient in food and about 20% of the population is in donor-supported social safety net program (Ibid).

Facilitating factors are those favouring conditions for the perpetuation of movement. *Constraining factors* discourage moving. For instance, only 65% of those moving from Ethiopia to other African countries have passports. (Kuschminder, K et al., 2012) The lack of a travel/identity document makes Ethiopian migrants vulnerable to abuse and exploitation.

> As well as their function in the migration process as outlined above – predisposing, proximate, precipitating, or mediating – these dimensions include locality, scale, duration and depth or tractability. (Van Hear, N et al., 2012)

Locality. Corridors of migration develop along multiple interconnected localities. What are those drivers which induce the perpetuation of movement? Migration is not centred around, for instance, the area of destination. The reason is that the process of migration involves multiple localities. For instance, Ethiopian migration starts in rural areas and the internal migration is not an isolated movement. Many Ethiopians looking to migrate internationally come from rural area. Then, the movement is perpetuated in urban area where Ethiopian migrants start their journey abroad. The perpetuation of movement goes through a series of consecutive and inter-related 'push-pull' stages of migration. Ethiopians migrate internally from rural to urban area to save money for going abroad. The movement goes through a series of other transformations pertaining to 'those drivers which operate transnationally or translocally, such as transnational labour markets' (Van Hear, N et al., 2012).

Scale. The movement could be characterized not only by 'different geographical scales' but, also, by different 'social scales', including a gender dimension. For instance, Ethiopian international migration is highly gendered.

Timeframe/duration. Migration patterns could be precipitated by unexpected political or economic decisions. Long-term drivers could induce bidirectional movements ('back and forth'). For instance, the recent election of Abyia Ahmed, the prime minister of Ethiopia, who embarked this country on a path of democracy, could reduce long-term migration and even determine Ethiopians living abroad to return home.

Depth or tractability. Ethiopia was unable to pull back diaspora (Hassan, S. and Negash, M. 2013) although recent economic reports evidenced a growing economy. Is this inability to reverse brain drain signalling a lack of effective policy action? Moreover, it is still unknown whether the recent political change in Ethiopia will 'operate on the surface of the society' (Van Hear, N et al. 2012) or act upon drivers 'that are more deeply embedded and intractable.' (Van Hear, N et al. 2012) The success of policy action depends on adjusting the depth or tractability of the intended change.

Both cases (i.e. Romanian and Polish migratory trends in the Northern hemisphere and Ethiopian migration in Sub-Saharan Africa) reveal a migration driven mainly by economic factors, which appear not to be an unexpected coincidence. Migratory patterns, geographically distributed in either the Northern or the Southern Hemisphere, bear the imprint of a migration regime rooted in a specificity of migratory trends, at least in the case of South-South migration.[1] For instance, Ethiopian migration exhibits a multi-stage approach: the first stages take place internally: Ethiopians choose to migrate from very poor rural areas to 'smaller cities to earn enough to go to Addis Ababa, and then save money to leave Ethiopia (Atnafu et al. 2014, p. 20, apud Carter, B. & Rohwerder, B., 2016, p. 15). The locality does make a difference within migratory processes in Sub-Saharan Africa. There is a dichotomy between poverty and place in apprehending a multiscalar dynamics of migration, an issue which will be further explored in the next chapter within the relation between multiscalar globalization and welfare regimes.

---

[1]   'Scholars on migration increasingly rely on the concept of migration regime to capture the relation between mobility, regulation and discourse.' (Rass, C. & Wolff, F., 2018)

CHAPTER III

GLOBALIZATION AND WELFARE REGIMES

We need to reconsider the relationship between types of 'multi-scalar dynamics', as in Sassen's approach (2010, p. 5), and variations of European welfare regimes. Globalization influences the dynamic of welfare regimes so that a critical examination of theoretical and methodological aspects of globalization processes is needed.

'Multi-scalar globalization' and 'ethno-globalization'

Whenever a certain pattern is affirmed at the global scale, it can also be considered a global-scale pattern. As nationality is such a pattern asserted at the global scale, we may consider it as a specific global pattern. When a national pattern contracts, we may speak of Sassen's (2003) 'denationalization' process. A pattern undergoes a pendulum swing like a cyclical two-phase movement: an upswing followed by a downswing. Paradoxically, the ascendant phase of a local-universal pattern is the temporal frame embedding the co-existential globalization, while a descendent phase of such a pattern becomes the temporal frame

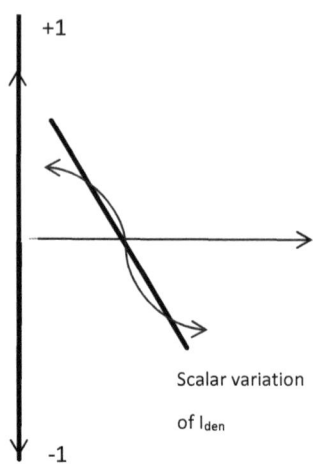

Scalar variation

of I_{den}

for hegemonic globalization. The historical process embeds within it these opposite processes. The national pattern is an example of co-existential globalization or, as it was called, ethno-globalization (cf. Badescu, 2008).

Another example of co-existential globalization is the rise of multiple civilizations at the global scale throughout history. Civilizations are revealed to stem from what is latently common to different groups of nations, who therefore share several archetypes. I consider civilizations also relevant to 'ethno-globalization' or, using another syntagma, to *co- existential globalization*. We have to take care not to make confusion between these notions and what Morrill, D., (1993), Howitt, R., (1993), Jonas, A., (1994), Brenner, N., (1998) presented as a 'multi-scalar globalization' with its specific locations (Sassen, 2003). Their approach had assumed the asymmetrical character of the globalization process and concept whereas we are required to invoke the same unique globalization process. We face here a twofold risk of absolutizing what Sassen calls 'scalar analytics' and of relativizing up to ignoring the 'historicity of scales' (Ibid, p. 2). Nevertheless, such a challenge does not refer only to the risk of the 'reification of national scale' but also to the risk of reification of the hegemonic global scale, ignoring not only the multiple globalizations but also the co-existential globalization. This globalization patterns embed both the particular, specific character and the global, universal span resulting into the rise of co-existing civilizations. The co-existential globalization permeates the process of the nationality affirmation. The nationality perpetuates two features: the *global type* and the *specific character*. It illustrates at the level of different nations the embedment of global into local, i.e. the intertwining of the global scale with the specific content, a phenomenon first revealed, as we have already mentioned, through the rise of civilizations.

The 'sites for globalization': denationalization index

THE EMBEDMENT OF THE GLOBAL INTO LOCAL LEADS TO THE EMERGENCE of what Sassen called 'site for globalization', that is, a *locus* which fosters the globalization while keeping its local character. Such 'places' locate cross-border (trans-boundary) networks which are the proper content of globalization be it of the hegemonic or of the co-existential type.

> Today, particular institutional components of the national state begin to act as the institutional home for the operation of powerful dynamics constitutive of what we could describe as 'global capital' and 'global capital markets'. In so doing, these state institutions contribute to reorient their particular policy work or, more broadly, state agendas towards the requirements of the global economy. This then raises a question about what is 'national' in these institutional components of states linked to the implementation and regulation of economic globalization. (Ibid, p. 22)

'A new normativity' (Ibid, p. 9) emerges due to a 'small number of state agencies, of legislative initiatives and executive orders' and because 'these strategic sectors run in complex interactions with private, transnational powerful actors' (Sassen, 2003, p. 22). The paradoxical effect of such a new normativity is the form devoid of substance marked by a disabled functioning (cf. Motru, C. R., 1904; Badescu, I., 2001; Badescu, I., Cucu-Oancea, O., 2011). It can induce the effect of denationalization although it fails to enhance the nation's substance. The new elite celebrate the form as if it was the new reality, while it appears to be a form devoid of substance. The norm of the balance between form and substance was destroyed because the equilibrium between the specific and the global was itself destroyed.

When the global side annihilates a specific character, we may speak of a destructive globalization. Globalization can devour specificity and locality, so we may speak about de-processing, a type of 'departiculization' and de-particularization of the system. De-particulization is a process through which 'a phenomenal particle-like character is supposed to decrease at the benefit of its process-like character'.[1] Concomitantly with de-particulization, an 'increase of temperature' is recorded in the system, a 'decrease of the relative mass, de-processing and de-gravitation' (Ibid). Along with de-particulization, globalization brings phenomena such as mass decreasing, de-processing and de-gravitation. Otherwise expressed, a certain pattern assumes a phenomenal particle-like character and a process-like character at the same time. Therefore, it might evolve into increasing or decreasing its phenomenal particle-like character at the benefit of its process-like character, and its inner balance can be destroyed depending on the external super-added influences. Had such super-added external influences lacked, the referred pattern keeps its balance between the two opposite pressures. Whenever such influences interfere, the pattern restores this imbalance. When the hegemonic globalization, for instance, stresses on the process-like character of a pattern, it causes a relative mass decreasing and de-gravitation, i.e. the decreasing of its specific gravitational force. All these phenomena go on within what Sassen used to call 'site for globalization', a *locus* which fosters the globalization along with or without devouring the specificity and locality phenomenon. We are entrusted to affirm that the first 'site for globalization', as Sassen calls it, is civilization, the second 'site for globalization' came to be, in modern times, nationality, so that, 'the subnational', as Sassen calls it, is but the third 'site for globalization'. All inner geopolitical entities can be considered as examples of what Sassen used to call *site for globalization*.

---

1   http://www.itmewewhy.com/properties_monocomplex_particle_departiculization.

Figure 1: *The frequency of situations affecting work or family responsibilities (%)*

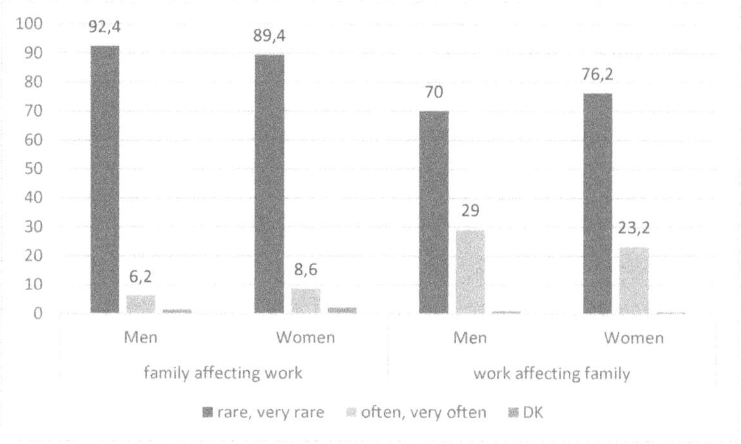

Source: Calculations due to Andra-Bertha Sanduleasa based on *Public Opinion Barometer's module 'Family*

'Scalar analytics' of denationalization process. The hysteresis effect-based forecasting

ANY CROSS-BORDER NETWORK AND PROCESS CAN BE ASSIMILATED TO different types of *sites for globalization*. A notorious example is migration. It was assumed that the volume of migration varies proportionally with the shortness of the distance. On the other hand, we must notice that activists involved in cross-border network make the embedment of long distances into local spaces possible through specific activities. It illustrates what we mean by internally induced denationalization. It happens so that while a certain phenomenon started to expand, it comes to actuate a self-generating character. That phenomenon begins to foster its own growth. Therefore, it grows proportionally with the radial distance (the long distance being included) ascribed to 'the number of opportunities at that destination'.[2] The equation of migration, therefore, might be rewritten based on the idea that the volume of migrants grows proportionally not only with short but also with long distance. Had *cross-border networks* encompassed *great*

_____

2   Mitali, V., 'General Theories of Migration – Explained!', Source: http://www.   yourarticlelibrary.com/population-geography/4-general-theories-of-migration- explained/43257 (accessed 24.07.2019) paraphrasing Stouffer's Theory of Mobility

spaces, then the volume of migration will grow proportionally with long as well as short distances. On the other hand, returning to the welfare regime issue, we may notice that whenever local labour groups opt for migration, they bring forth a welfare experience gained abroad within a national welfare state so that, finally, the local embeds the international. We may assimilate such a phenomenon with the denationalization process, so we also may conclude that denationalization grows proportionally with the amplitude of such processes of embedding, for instance, international welfare experiences into local. The equation of denationalization can be conceived in this example as follows (cf. Badescu & Badescu, 2014):

$Id_n = f(VM, D, Net)$, where:

Id_n = denationalization index; VM = volume of migration;

D = long distance;

Net = cross-border networks or geographical channels of migration.

Migration patterns bring in a certain denationalization (to a certain degree). It is important to keep in mind that denationalization gets through nested intervals and, consequently followed by as many counter-reactions. These kinds of reactions are impacted by anti-conversion movements. Therefore, denationalization is but a B-phase manifestation of a cyclical up-and-down movement and we may apprehend it only by considering the parameters of this B-phase along with the parameters that prevail in A-phase.

We may use a Hofstadter type of index as follows:

$Idn = (F_p - F_a)(100 - F_o)/100$, where:

Idn = Scalar Index of denationalization;

F_p = number (frequency) of those with pro-system (pro-globalization, in our example) options;

F_a = number (frequency) of those with anti-system options (called in A-phase the resistant to the expansion of the system, that is, to the hegemonic globalization);

F_o = the frequency of those who get an indifferent attitude (neither opt for the system nor reject it.

Applied to the migrants in quest for welfare the new index form can be rewritten in this way:

Idn = $(N_p - N_a)$ (100-N_o) /100, where:

N_p = volume of those who have already opted for migration or do express their intention to migrate in quest for a new welfare experience;

N_a = number of those who reject the migration alternative as a path towards a new welfare experience;

N_o = number of those who declare themselves to be indifferent (neither opt for this path towards a new welfare experience nor reject such an alternative). Aiming at evaluating anchor points on the European multiple scale of welfare regimes we arrived at an *average index* as following:

$\Sigma f_i p_i / \Sigma f_i$, where: $\Sigma f_i p_i$ = frequency of those who are in quest for a new welfare experience through migration; Σf_i = the whole population under investigation.

The first variation is between -1 and +1 while the second is between 0 and 1. It appears that the variation of index is a cyclical one: throughout B-phase the index of denationalization varies upward and during A-phase it is moving downward, allowing for the opposite movement of re-nationalization (towards enhancing the national trend and orientation). We may speak about a *hysteresis effect*, being that the index variation depends on the cyclical phase. *It shifts the meaning into opposite directions depending on the cyclical phase.* An ascendant variation is accompanied by a denationalization process and a descendent variation produces the frame for a re-nationalization process. The hysteresis effect is the main argument for using this index for the forecasting operation. It is obvious that, as long as it lasts, a cyclical phase will induce its related process. There is a response lag within the forecasted process. As a matter of fact, denationalization is a deficiency, that is, 'a state of being behind or late'. It is the measure of deficit produced by the cyclical B-phase. We are faced with a hysteresis-based forecasting operation. We are entrusted to believe such a particular cycle is universal although it lacks a Kondratieff periodicity. Its universality ensues from the peculiarity of social and cultural pattern aiming at attaining a global scale. Such an aspiration equates with an awakening of that inner dualism proper to any cyclical phenomenon. Let us draw the *variation profile of Scalar index of denationalization/renationalization* as it results from the theoretical scalar pattern.

The self-centred welfare experiences are in negative variation while the area of positive variation is assigned to the quest for new welfare as experienced by actors of denationalization processes.

Global scaling and lateral scaling

Let us resume the traits of Sassen's (2003) concept of 'site for globalization'. Sassen leads us to consider, while approaching globalization, not only what is 'global in scale' but also the 'locally scaled practices and conditions articulated to global dynamics' (Sassen, 2007, p. 7) and the 'multiplication of cross-border connections among various localities fed by the recurrence of certain conditions across localities' (Sassen, 2003, p. 3). This peculiarity of globally scaled dynamics being embedded in and with local, national, subnational practices and conditions points to 'site for globalization'. The intertwining of the local practices and conditions with the global dynamics transforms their locus in a *site for globalization*. The local practices and conditions do not hold by themselves, not even potentially, the feature of being a site for globalization.

Therefore, all that transcends local boundaries which entail or are cross-border connections among various countries and 'localities', appears to be a sign of the 'recurrence of certain conditions across localities' (Sassen, 2003, p. 3). Those recurrent conditions across localities are the content of what Sassen calls a *site for globalization*. The site for globalization is a locus (a place, a local elite, a social or cultural segment, a certain business etc.) where global dynamics are embedded in the local scaling entailing recurrent conditions across localities, countries, etc. A site for globalization is a locus where isotropic or anisotropic scaling (transformations at varied scales) run their course. Isotropy is a transformation that is a 'function of radius only [...] with no preferred axis for other physical attributes'.[3] Isotropy implies that 'scaling exponents are the same in all directions' (Lovejoy, S. et al., 2007). When this 'scale factor' is different for different axis directions of the transformation process we speak about anisotropic scaling. I used to call it *lateral scaling*, being that such a process induces a shift of an object's gravitational centre. It becomes a subalternated object. Hegemonic scaling induces such effects, so we may speak in this case about a *lateral scaling* affecting a nation or even a *civilization*. As Sassen says: 'the global capital market is constituted both through electronic markets with global span, and through locally embedded conditions, i.e. financial centres and all they entail, from infrastructure to systems of trust' (Sassen, S., 2003, p. 3). Therefore, the system cannot solve the problem of harmonization of these different scaling within its complex dynamic by itself. As actors of system, we are supposed to be able to bring into unity what is logically contradictory as if our thought might rely in its processing on the principle of 'included third' (*tertium datur*) while we know that the pivotal logical prop is the principle of the excluded third (*tertium non datur*). As a matter of fact, we learned to include logical contradictions into spiritual unity because our way of collective life is based on such types of unified and unifying structures. Civilizations and nationality account for such spiritual units as they reveal being able to unify the opposed scaling. Beyond the nationality and civilization as a possible way toward spiritual unity, we need to add other factors and sources of and for harmonization like the family. A Public Opinion Barometer on the 'Family Life' reveals the role played by family as a source of satisfaction with life and as a factor of harmonizing different social sectors of life. The data shows that work affects family more than the other way around. The data is shown in Figure 1, on the next page.

It is obvious that family is a favouring filter for the inner balance of people, while work cannot play the same role. The family exerts its lateral scaling on globalization although it appears to lack strength for such a role. Therefore, we may conclude that family plays a positive role in the domestic

---

3   The Isotropic Universe, Cambridge University Press 1999, Source: https://ned.ipac.caltech.edu/level5/Peacock/Peacock3_1.html (accessed 24.07.19)

dynamics of welfare experiences, so that if we consider its supportive role, we shall correct the variation model of welfare regimes. It is a suggestive example for the power of small communities to start lateral scaling of the global. There are issues in the system which the actors of the system could not properly solve. Such a problem refers to the challenge and imperative exigency of unifying the richness with poverty, luxury with scarcity, within a certain reference (family, nation or even an entire civilization).

Northern Europe learned to tackle this issue by inventing different welfare regimes. Two ways of dealing with such a challenge emerged at the European scale: the Northern Christian capitalist pattern based on what Weber called *in-worldly (intra-mundane) asceticism*, and the *civil wars*, i.e. the war of a powerful nation against a weaker one ending by subjugating it and by subalternizing local elites. Such a system is known in history as *colonialism*. While the first path leads to the affirmation of nationality at the scale of the already powerful nations, the second leads to denationalization so that certain people or groups of people are pushed by the very logic of the modern world system into a peripheral condition. There emerges a geo- economic stratified system compounded of centres, semi-peripheries and peripheries (cf. Wallerstein, 1984).

Therefore, the global scaling evolves on the local, national, sub-national sites being articulated with local contradictory scaling, the denationalizing scaling being included as the most relevant example.

From 'scalar analytics' to welfare regime analysis

ONE WAY TOWARDS DENATIONALIZATION IS TO TAKE OUT THE 'subnational places' and to put them in the service of global or lateral scaling. This path includes not only places but local elites and entire social segments of a society like the segment of migrants in quest for jobs and welfare.

Therefore, Western welfare regimes become 'sites for globalization' once they become reference points for local aspirations. Such places, for instance the ones Sassen used to call 'global cities', along with their social segments, become places where 'multiple global circuits intersect' (Sassen, S., 2003, p. 4). Such an intersection re-positions them 'on several structured cross-border geographies, each typically with distinct scopes and constituted in terms of distinct practices and actors' (Ibid). There emerge, in this way, different inner geopolitical arrangements that foster different denationalizing processes. Denationalization comes not only from external factors and geopolitical entities but also from such inner geopolitical entities. 'Global cities', subalternized elites, 'subnational places' (global cities being included in this typological group) are all examples for what we denote by inner geopolitical entities.

The aubalternated elite, for instance, plays a role which is linked more closely to the global dominant élite than to the nation upon which it is exercising its ruling role. In the South-Eastern European area, we may distinguish the historical alternation of subalternated elites and of auto-centred elites so that the historical process in the area is a bizarre alternation of denationalizing phases with re-nationalizing phases. We may speak of a cyclical alternation of socially conquest and re-conquest phases. Moreover, we need to also consider what Sassen used to call 'lateral scaling', i.e. the processes triggered by cross-bordering and/or metropolitan actors to subalternate different social groups and even people to their own interest. The globalization itself, bearing on a hegemonic character, induces *a lateral scaling* (anisotropic scaling that changes radically the shape of a social group, a nation etc.) The site for globalization – be it national or subnational – appears to be overloaded with strains and contradictions so that for local people the globalization is fatally a contradictory process, a process full of contradictions. Such contradictions entail problems that challenge local elites to look for solutions based on that kind of solving pattern which involves a global response embedded into a locally oriented response.

Denationalization is also a shift of 'theorization logic' in the mind of local elites. They end up by thinking with the logic of globalization, totally ignoring the logic of the local being it a local community, a nation or even a civilization. A gap between legal country and real country emerges, that is between lower class people and people from upper class as if they belong to different nations. We face the phenomenon of two nations in one and with the sign of a tragic failure of local elites to find out solution that embed the *global challenge* into a *local logic*. This is one side of denationalization. Let us resume: a typical process of denationalization is the segmentation of the people, leading to the emergence of two societies in one, over there where it was, usually, one.

A sort of hyper-penalizing state provokes a 'rupture between the government and governed' (Meyer, J. A., 1976). It is enough to wage a political war against different factions within a certain society under the excuse of a war against corruption, for instance, leading, finally, to such a rupture.

The two types of state, the 'deep state' (Lofgren, 2014, p. 1) and hyper-penalizing state cannot induce allegiance and trust, so they act as a factor of denationalization not of enhancing the forces of nationality.

On the other hand, nationality and the nation are not merely part of 'nested hierarchies of scale running from local to the international' but an ethno-spiritual, ethno-social frame with 'a continuous global span'. Moreover, the nation as a collective unit includes, Sassen argues, different entities that embed global dynamics. One example is that of the 'global cities', as Sassen called them, places where global dynamics are embedded. These cities seem to be 'sub-national places where multiple global circuits intersect' (Sassen, S., 2003, p. 4) so they are part of a nation unit and, on the same time, part of different 'cross-border geographies' (Ibid). They reveal to be sites for globalization as they become places where a growing number of 'cross-border circuits' (Ibid, p. 3) are more and more articulated. Nations must learn how to manage such global dynamics to protect themselves. Nation becomes from now on a site for globalization and can keep its attribute of being a nation only if its elites learn to run those growing number of cross-border circuits, those global dynamics which are embedded in microenvironments of its encompassing frame. One of these cross-border circuits is the migration being that migrants are looking for a different welfare experience. By result, migration as a process produces a network of different welfare experiences so that beneath the national geography there emerge a *European geography of the welfare experience network* and we need to apprehend the welfare issue based on a proper method which *combines scalar analytics with cluster analysis*. This is one global or transnational issue that governmental elites need to deal with in the process of globalization. It equates with gaining competence for local running of global politics.

In some instances (cf. Ibid), cases in successful 'global politics' through local entities (institutions, places, microenvironments, firms, interactive technologies, activist organizations etc.) were invoked. Such local entities with a global span are, on the same time, part of nation as collective unit, part of cross-border circuits, and local elites need to assume their ambivalence. They must learn to administer these types of entities and processes induced by such cross-border circuits. One local élite passes the national exam only if it has learned how to administer global dynamics, cross- border circuits and sub-national entities with global span. The responsibility for the preservation of a national entity and unity falls on the national elites. It depends on them and on their capability to avoid the risks of denationalization and finally of national disintegration.

PART III

THE FOURTH CAPITALISM

CHAPTER I

THE RISE AND FALL OF
'WELFARE CAPITALISM':
HISTORICISM AND UNIVERSALISM
IN CAPITALISM

Capitalist formations successively coexist

WELFARE IS ROOTED IN WESTERN CAPITALISM. IN EXPLAINING the origin and variation of welfare regimes, it is necessary to note that they form part of a larger reference framework, which Esping-Andersen called 'welfare capitalism'. The welfare dynamic results from the dynamic of capitalism. Comprehending the welfare dynamic reclaims the understanding of the dynamic of capitalism. To explain the essence of capitalism is equivalent to looking for a proper answer to the paradoxical aspect of the rise of capitalism. The paradox is the particularity of something being at the same time relative, i.e. particular in manifestation and universal constituting its essence. We are led to note that capitalism is, at the same time, historical in its manifestation and trans-historical in its essence, successive (evolutionary) and co-existent, pluralist and universal. If we search for a way of understanding society, we may comprehend how the society and economy of *evolutionary capitalism* coexists with *universalist capitalism*. How is it possible that evolutionary, i.e. *relative capitalism*, is also a *universalist capitalism*, so that they finally become a universalized capitalism? History is a 'natural lecture' on such a challenging issue. Deleuze and Guattari call upon such a paradoxical aspect of capitalism. Evolutionary capitalism equates to a pluralist capitalism, meaning that a certain type of capitalism is successively co-existent with another type of capitalism. Or, as Lampert, J. argues: 'social formations can co-exist extrinsically in succession, or intrinsically and jointly, i.e. by speed or delay respectively' (2006, p. 159). He calls this phenomenon 'meta-consistency' presenting it under those two types. 'The tricky thing is that one of the two socio-temporal forms that co-exist is succession and the other is co-existence' (Ibid) so they contend with each other to promote their own perspective on thinking the phenomenon and the 'previousness' of one relative to the other (the former retaining the pre-eminence as to the definition of the latter) does not annul their contemporaneity.[1]

> In the 'transition' from state to capitalism, for the first time in history, the before and the after of an event are 'co-existing poles' rather than 'stages'. (Ibid)

Three philosophers (Deleuze, Guattari and Lampert) describe such a paradoxical phenomenon of a succession to also a co-existence invoking what called 'the capture paradigm'.[2] They underline the reality nature of the paradigm as it is even itself this 'capture paradigm'. The paradigms as natural phenomena are intrinsic guides of either doing or interpreting something. There is in history, a phenomenon of historical capturing as the three philosophers argued.

What is interesting for us is the kind of consistency

---

1   'Social formations can co-exist under two types of what I am calling meta- consistency: extrinsically in succession, or intrinsically and jointly, i.e. by speed or delay respectively. As always, the tricky thing is that one of the two socio-temporal forms that co-exist is succession and the other is co-existence. When a society structured by succession co-exists with a society structured by co-existence, the previousness of the former relative to the later (as defined by the former) is concurrent with the contemporaneity of the two (as defined by the latter).' (Lampert, Jay, 2006, p. 159).

2   '[When] successor turns the prior social formation into its predecessor by turning succession into co-existence, capturing historical succession' (Lampert, Jay, 2006, p. 159).

where historical succession as such is captured by the state.[3] 'Insofar as the state is not staggered but is the simultanization of economic functions (555), it is the paradigmatic regime, the regimated regime, whose essence is to be a code. This is another way of saying that the state originates when succession becomes co-existence. The origin of the third historical epoch, capitalism, is thus 'internal' to its own processes, as the state is, but, unlike the state, Deleuze and Guattari say, capitalism 'evolves' or 'mutates', accumulating self-causality (560). [...] The state [...] constantly releases free particles of wealth and labour. These escapees normally get recaptured, but until they do, they operate as proto-capitalist fluxes, which in turn release temporal particles into the third stage and type of history, which I will call the history of 'release' (560).
(Lampert, J., 2006, p. 162)

The entire explanation of the dynamic of capitalism consists in comprehending the fact that such a dynamic is capturing a relation between state and capitalism, so that the capitalism reveals itself as an expression and as a measure of a releasing process. Capitalism originates in such an embedded form, as an engrafted capitalism. It is obvious that the relation between state and capitalism, as a relation between 'releasing' and 'recapturing', appears to be the nucleus where the 'welfare capitalism' (Esping-Andersen) itself springs from. 'The wealth has to break away from ruling functionaries' (Lampert, J., 2006) in order to multiply, to increase and proliferate, but it has to be 'recaptured' (Lampert, J., 2006) to take shape of a new process called social redistribution and to become the source of the welfare state. And, moreover, these two successive processes must co-exist. Only in this way the wealth may play a double role: of simultaneously being the source of profit and of the welfare. We called that type of capitalism highly harmonized with the state and

---

3   (d) "'Intrinsic" meta-consistency - the capture paradigm (544-5): This is the main topic of the Plateau: a successor turns the prior social formation into its predecessor by turning succession into co-existence, capturing historical succession. What is important for us are not "powers of appropriation" (e.g. taking over existing gold mines), or "powers to be transferred" (taking over existing armies). What is interesting for us is the kind of consistency where historical succession as such is captured by the state' (Lampert, Jay, 2006, p. 159).

family, operating as a medium of the harmonization of the two opposite processes – of releasing and of re-capturing wealth – and because of its own intrinsic dynamisms, the fourth capitalism. It is, par excellence, the continuous confirmation of the co-existence of successions, i.e. of the two mentioned successive processes (of releasing and capturing), and nothing from outside of its own functioning could ever stop its perpetuation and equilibrium.

> For capitalism to exist, wealth has to break away from ruling functionaries and attach itself to fluid labour power, liquid investments, and uncharted markets. (Lampert, J., 2006, p. 162)

The wealth had to break away from 'ruling functionaries' and 'attach itself to fluid labour power, liquid investment' (Ibid) to arrive at a 'model of realisation', becoming *'la raison d'etre'* of capitalism. Further on, this multiplied wealth has to be released by the capitalist system itself to serve another function and purpose: the growth of civilization and general welfare. Should such an operation be possible, a new economic behaviour had to emerge. This new capitalist behaviour had to be oriented toward the quest for profit and towards a general purpose that the Northern Christian capitalists used to ordain *ad maiorem Dei Gloriam* (*'To the greater glory of God'*). They put the accumulated wealth in the service of a superior purpose: the growth of general civilization. A rational capitalism based on the labour rationalization as a way of increasing the profit *ad maiorem Dei Gloria (To the greater glory of God)* emerged.

> The conditions of accumulated wealth and labour are not the cause of capitalism. They are conditions that allow economic events to occur in free encounters; capitalism is proximally contingent on these encounters, not on the conditions for these encounters. Capitalism preserves the instability of the elements that drive it, simply by forcing them to co- exist. (Ibid, p. 163)

History itself was re-captured and so what is transient becomes perennial for the successions to co-exist and instable elements to be part as working elements of a stable system. Such a miraculous becoming has taken place where something spiritually extraordinary happened.

Max Weber accounted such a historical miracle to a civilizational dense area: Christian Northern Europe. Let us examine critically the notorious theories on the topic.

Co-existing Civilizational Capitalism

WE ENCOUNTERED THE WEBERIAN MODE OF RATIONALIZING AN economic system deeply rooted into complex, intertwined culturally, religiously and even socially induced 'models of realization' arising at a 'different rate of speed in each realization'.[4] Thus, we believe the emergence of the so-called Nordic type of capitalist system happened at a different rate when comparing the British capitalism with the other Nordic states' capitalist systems. We may call upon the highest speed rate in the realization of the British capitalist model and the main cause for such high speed is the Industrial Revolution whose territoriality proved to be hegemonic. We may, also, conclude upon the 'paradigmatic regime' of the British-mode of realization of the meta-capitalist regime whose main premises were deeply rooted not only in the 'rationalist' capitalist system but, above all, in its subjectified form deeply rooted in the hegemonic presence of British 'moral imperialism'. I concluded that the co-existence of British moral imperialism and Northern Calvinist capitalism played the decisive role of inducing, at the same time, a fairly high rate of speed of a certain realization (to allow for innovative behaviour to escape from the compulsive historical forces) and a fairly anchoring power to make stable such a 'model of realization' in order to make possible a miracle to break through the very determinist historical evolution.

The rise and fall of the British Empire brought about several globalizing

---

4   'Deleuze and Guattari propose an analogy with axioms applied to heterogeneous fields. Some states may be easier for capitalism to apply to, but capitalism is capable of using everything from regime change to space travel, not to mention virtually every form of production. The applications describe a *"ritournelle"* around "models of realization" (567 – 70). This may not explain why capitalism arises in certain places at particular times, but it might explain how it arises at a different rate of speed in each realization. Realizations of capitalism are relayed temporally as well as structurally from state to state.' (Lampert, J., 2006: 164)

effects, including 'distinct patterns of migration and communication, critical shifts in the movement of goods and capital, new forms of transnational connection, changing conceptualizations of community and individual rights, and discrete forms of violence and conflict that outlasted the 'formal' end of empires.' (Thomas, M., Thompson, A., 2013) A new collective behaviour emerged because of such globalizing effects. Historically, the fourth capitalism originated in the double structural precondition that only British moral imperialism allowed for a new collective behaviour while the Northern Christian behaviour allowed wealth to escape from capitalist coercing forces.

The capitalism of the predestination doctrine (Calvinism) co-exists with the capitalism of 'moral imperialism'

THE CAPITALISM OF THE DOCTRINE OF PREDESTINATION (CALVINISM), which is the essence of the Nordic countries' system, *successively co-exists* with the capitalism of 'moral imperialism' (i.e. Victorian type). Such a historical coexistence evolved in Europe and only for its Northern Christian area, explaining why welfare capitalism emerged. It is now evident that it is the very nucleus of the fourth capitalism which is purposely a civilizational capitalism, being that it emerged from a creative economy (as its medium and at the same time as its result). This is the third definitional condition of its historical possibility.

Let us summarize those three conditions that made possible the emergence of the fourth capitalism: the co-existence of successions, creative economy and dual oriented capitalism: towards both the increase of profit and the growth of welfare state. The last feature is a definitional trait for what is called the civilizational capitalism. The co-existence of successions, the creative economy and the civilizational capitalism (oriented also towards the development of a new historical civilization) represent the three dimensions of the fourth capitalist paradigm.

The historical capitalist paradigms were rather regarded in a typological light as Hirschman called for 'types of development theories', claiming there are 'two unified systems of thought', i.e. *orthodox economics* and *neo-Marxism.* Each one of these two branches of economic thought have its main determinant of conferring the pattern or the logical construct, founding each theoretical perspective.

One of the orthodox position's theorems 'is that in a market economy, benefits flow to all participants, be they individuals or countries, from all voluntary acts of economic intercourse ("or else they would not engage in those acts")' (Hirschman, A., 2013, p. 52).

The neo-Marxists claimed that 'exploitation or "unequal exchange"' (Ibid) gives the particularity of a capitalist system whose main historical determination is based on a 'long process of exploitation' or a selfish mode of redistributing the added value in a society. Major social, economic and political events witnessed the rise of these two major capitalist paradigms during the 19th century. There is a third economic paradigm framed into what I have called the fourth capitalism as its main feature – the structural dualism of being at the same time the medium and the result of a new economic behaviour, oriented concurrently toward the growth of profit and toward the expansion of welfare state. The three paradigms have co-existed throughout the modern era.

The Victorian epoch marked not only the development of the UK over more than a century, but also the advance of the Industrial Revolution and the definitive anchorage of the fourth capitalism in the Northern European area, which has become, due to this circumstance, the core-area of the modern capitalism.

Victorian moral values can be regarded as a correlating with the Weberian ethos and therefore as a second nucleic condition of the fourth capitalism. The ethos of the Victorian era has deep roots in the Victorian society where religion used to be a 'dominant interest [...], impacting almost every aspect of life and culture' (Melnyk, J., 2008).[5]

---

5   Church attendance was as high as 50%. As Erickson notes, 'Biblical Christianity was thickly intertwined in the fabric of Victorian society'. Christian symbols were prominently displayed everywhere, such as signs reading "choose this day whom you will serve," and "be sure your sins will find you out" on prison walls. English men and women were "serious about their faith," which "undergirded their lives to an extent unimaginable to nonchurchgoers in our own time." (Carolly Erickson, Her Little Majesty: The Life of Queen Victoria (New York:

We may see similarities between the ways the Victorian ethos and the Protestant ethic (cf. Weber, M., 2010) were formed and, moreover, contributed to the development of an early new type of the capitalism system. We tempt to believe that the basis in the protestant theology that significantly contributed to the social success and wealth of the classes in 'rational' capitalism was similar to the theology of the Victorian era that contributed to the advance of the British Empire, the success of the Industrial Revolution and to the anchorage of the fourth capitalism in history. The protestant theology was the mouthpiece of a 'rational' capitalist system that was later in charge with the advance of the German typology of the modern capitalist system, while the ethos of a triumphalist epoch known as the *Victorian era* became the proper justification of the British typology of Weberian 'rational' capitalism. Therefore, we may depict two conjoint typologies of the historical capitalism: Calvinist capitalism and Victorian capitalism. Their co-existence made possible the emergence and the anchorage of the fourth capitalism in the world history.

The meta-regime nature of historical capitalism and the 'mainstream economics'

THE BENEFITS OF BRITISH INDUSTRIALISM AS A WORLD NOVELTY HAVE spread over the entire world, marking a new era in universal history. It is true, on the other hand, that the spread of the benefits of the early British Industrialism were rather unevenly distributed in a world whose geopolitical frontiers were shaped through the dominance of the British Empire.

In the meantime, the proponents of 'laissez-faire' capitalism (Physiocrats - Vincent de Gournay, Francois Quesnay, Turgot, Baron de L'Aulne), classical economists (Adam Smith, James Mill, David Ricardo) advocated the aspirational ideals of economic liberalism that later contributed to the emergence of 'mainstream economics' and therefore of the new way of thinking society and economy, that is, the new paradigm in economics and social science.

Simon & Schuster, 1997).

Moreover, mainstream economics would later contribute to the formation of the positivist paradigm, based on two assumptions: 'realist ontology' and 'representational epistemology', the origin of this paradigm being, usually, credited to Descartes (Robert Wood Johnson Foundation). There is a tendency towards narrowing the economic tradition in a way that would move the positivist paradigm centre stage and peripheralize the neo- Marxist doctrine as recognition of the demise of the communist regimes in the Central and Eastern Europe. The Fall of the Wall along with such major social breakthroughs that took place in Eastern Europe in 1989-1990 marked a turning point in the theoretical development, contributing, at least indirectly, to the advance of so-called 'mainstream economics'.

The classical economic tradition was based on the premise that the supply can create its own demand.[6] Keynes proposed his own theoretical perspective to 'classical economics', arguing that 'the second, strong form of Say's Law only holds if increases in individual savings exactly match an increase in aggregate investment' (Keynes, J. M., 2007).[7] Keynes' own perspective underlined that the aggregate demand should be stimulated by government spending, an idea that proved to be anchored into reality during World War II (WW2) and in the following period in the US economy. The triumph of the Keynesian doctrine proved by the advance of US economy in the decades following WW2 is marking the debut of the new *sub-type* of the co-existing civilizational capitalism that had its roots in the new philosophy of indebtedness. Anyway, everything that has happened in the economy until now appears to be a continuous demonstration of the progressive advance of what I call the fourth capitalism, that is a capitalism which makes of creative economy, co-existence of successions and civilizational capitalism its own defining dimensions. By such an adaptive selection, the affirmation of the fourth capitalism becomes the most significant event on the global scale of human history. The co-existence of successions is illustrated by an event memorized as the Breton Woods agreement. Let us explain.

---

6   Say's Law
7   cf. *General Theory*, Ch.1,2

A new 'post-bellum era'

THE BRETTON WOODS AGREEMENT PAVED THE WAY TOWARDS THE NEW 'regimated regime' – or the meta-regime of historical capitalism – whose main premise is that all 'models of realization' of historical capitalism continued to co-exist in the post-WW2 period. The paradigmatic pattern of evolutionary capitalism based on the Weberian ethos has been transposed into a new 'post-bellum era'. The transposition of the historical roots of evolutionary capitalism into the new era whose main discourse was marked by Keynesian doctrine has contributed to filtering patterns of capitalism. The transposition of historical roots of capitalist system could not necessarily imply that such conditions would have lost their historicity. Evolutionary capitalism has started to co-exist with the new capitalism proper to the new epoch. The post-war economic growth (1946-1960) marked this new era that might be regarded as well as a new way of co-existent manifestation of the 'models of realization' of the historical capitalism.

The Weberian ethos regarded as the main driver of historical capitalism, along with the doctrinarian way of its realization, impacted the post-war economic period. As a matter of fact, the evolution of capitalism, 'meta-regimated' by its paradigmatic pattern, takes the form of a process of moving away from the equilibrium (cf. Wallerstein, I., 2011). The epoch is characterized by the co-existence of at least three 'models of realization' of evolutionary capitalism: financial banking capitalism, industrial classic capitalism and welfare capitalism that is but a frontstage of the backstage fourth capitalism.

On the financial economy's 'looking-glass self'

FRACTIONAL RESERVE BANKING PROVIDES THE PRACTICAL JUSTIFICATION for what Wallerstein (2011) considered the process through which capitalism not only moves away from equilibrium but also bifurcates. Such a bifurcation in the developing of capitalist system triggered alternatives like the debt mechanisms which is mediated through the process of money creation.

We shall reveal such a mechanism to technically explain a boundaryless manifestation of business spaces mediated by the banking system. *The banking induces disorganized 'models of representation' in the capitalist world, as the fractional reserve banking becomes manifest through the mechanisms of indebtedness.* The process of repaying a certain amount of debt at a certain moment in time requires an additional value that is mediated by the creation of loanable funds.

Graham Towers, Governor of the Bank of Canada from 1935 to 1955, says: 'They (commercial banks), by their activities in making loans and investments, create liabilities for themselves, and call these liabilities '"eposits"' (Towers, Graham, 1939, cited in Jaikaran, J. S., 1992, p. 127). We are requested to add clarifications at this point. First, such types of liabilities are created by virtue of 'fractional reserve banking'. Second, commercial banks can multiply existing funds, including clients' deposits which, at the time when such deposits were created bore a promise to repay it **plus** interest. It is, somehow, similar to a loan where the amount of money being borrowed represents the principal whereas the loan is given in exchange for an interest which is paid back on top of the principal. Only that, when speaking about deposits, *ex ante*, i.e. before granting the loan, the client lends the money to the bank, expecting an interest on that deposit, in exchange. There is not only the bank that is lending depositors' money but, also, depositors themselves lend their own savings to banks in exchange for interest. The mechanism through which depositors facilitate the creation of a monetary base for money creation through the mechanism of fractional reserve banking needs further developments.

The operation of opening a deposit account requires a double entry accounting operation: first, the deposit is recorded as a liability. It means that the bank is held liable for the newly created bank deposit. The bank did not earn this money. The depositor is the owner. The money is credited into bank's account. These are demand and savings deposits. Second and simultaneously, the same amount of money appears as added asset ('debit') into bank's account. It is considered as money and used in the process of multiplication through the fractional reserve system. The bank can now use the new money deposited into its account for creating loans. This time, the bank uses its capability of multiplying money through fractional reserve system.

The money multiplied in the system through such multiplying mechanisms could be denoted as *fractional deposits*. The reason for calling it 'fractional' is that the initial deposit used in the money multiplier process represents only a fraction of the entire amount created in the form of loanable funds. Money created through the fractional reserve system leads to a new expanded monetary base which not only bears the imprint of the multiplication process but, foremost, represent a multiplication of the initial deposit (i.e. demand and savings deposit). The new money created is similar to scriptural money only that it was created through a separation (fractionation) process.

Banks have this unique capability in the economy, enabling them to create money through the process of multiplying their clients' deposits into *liabilities* '*deposits*'. Banks create money by virtue of multiplying such 'liabilities' into the banking system. Banks pay interest in exchange but only for using the money deposited into bank's account although a *premium* should be added on top of the existing deposit's interest rate. I identified two conditions to comprehend an expanded perspective on the interest-bearing account as follows:

    a. First, there is the condition of having an interest-bearing account. The interest rate is calculated based on the balance of the existing account;

    b. Second and because of the previous condition, the mechanism through which banks create money presupposes that the balance of existing saving accounts creates the base for the multiplication process in the banking system. A premium, i.e. added interest should be derived from this new condition.

It has become evident that banks' spread[8] is mostly facilitated by 'the

---

8   'Bank spread is the difference between the interest rate that a bank charges a borrower and the interest rate a bank pays a depositor. Also called the net interest spread, the bank spread is a percentage that tells someone how much money the

fact that banks technically face no limits to increasing the stocks of loans and deposits instantaneously' (Jakab, Z., Kumhof, M., 2015, p. iii).

Not incidentally, the Bank of England (2015) issued a working paper, arguing that 'the quantity of reserves is therefore a consequence, not a cause, of lending and money creation' (Jakab, Z., Kumhof, M., 2015, p. iii). Such an argument creates a false and dangerous primacy of bank's lending power. Bank of England experts (2014; 2015) start their argument from an arguable point: 'Saving does not by itself increase the deposits or 'funds available' for banks to lend' (McLeay, M. et al., 2014), although the authors of the Bank of England's report (2015) admit that 'lending starts with banks collecting deposits of real savings from one agent and ends with the lending of those savings to another agent' (Jakab, Z., Kumhof, M., 2015, p. 3).

The report issued by the Bank of England (2015) reviews main theoretical models, one argument being that 'new loans lead to deposit creation, not vice versa' (Ibid, p. 6).

> Lord Adair Turner (2013), former head of the UK Financial Services Authority: 'Banks do not, as many textbooks still suggest, take deposits of existing money from savers and lend it out to borrowers: they create credit and money ex nihilo — extending a loan to the borrower and simultaneously crediting the borrower's money account.' (Pozsar, 2014, cited in Jakab, Z., Kumhof, M., 2015, p. 6)

This last affirmation contradicts one simple, fundamental, and undeniable issue: the bank needs to hold a fraction ('reserve balances') of *its total* deposits with the central bank. It is hard to believe that banks create credit and money only by 'extending a loan to the borrower and simultaneously crediting the borrower's money account.' (Ibid) The mechanism of fractional reserve banking implies, also, creating credit and money *ex nihilo* by multiplying the existing money deposited by savers. Accepting that banks do not take deposits from savers then, we would presumably admit that the deposits from non-monetary financial

---

bank earns versus how much it gives out.' (Bank spread, https://www.bankrate.com/glossary/b/bank-spread)

institutions (i.e. representing 71% (2015) of total banking assets in the EU (EBF Facts & Figures 2016)) are not accounted for in the process of fractional reserve, which is an argument difficult to admit.'

In conclusion, fractional reserve banking is not a process of creating credit out of thin air as falsely admitted by the authors of Bank of England reports (2014; 2015). Deposits from non-monetary institutions are held and, foremost, used in the process of money creation. The interest paid to holders of deposits needs to be augmented to compensate for the condition of using such loanable funds[9] in the process of money creation. The mechanism through which savings account holders need to be recompensed for creating the condition for the bank(s) to multiply their initial savings/deposits within the process of fractional reserve will be further developed in a standalone research project.

It has become evident that mechanisms of fractional reserve banking create imbalances in terms of sharing benefits among those involved in the process of value creation in the economy. It appears to us that banks are privileged in the process of money creation, allowing for huge discrepancies in the process of profit allocation between agents involved in the process of money creation. Saving account holders are rewarded with interest only for the amount initially involved in the multiplication process. Banks multiply such initial funds in the process of loanable funds creation, charging interest rates on the volume of credit engaged, hence resulting in the process of money creation. The disproportion between factor payments becomes evident when comparing income from interest received by account holders, on one hand, and, conversely, the interest earned by banks in the process of credit expansion through fractional reserve banking.

The account holders are rewarded only for a tiny part, the visible proportion of loanable funds created, hence induced by the money held in their accounts. The invisible part is much larger than the visible proportion (i.e. the money held in bank accounts). It finally bears the imprint of a hidden disequilibrium in terms of factor payments.

---

9   'The term loanable funds include all forms of credit, such as loans, bonds, or savings deposits.'

Lacking a state of equilibrium in the economy could pave the way towards a dis-organized form of allocating resources in the economy. The resources in the economy are allocated based on a multitude of equilibrium prices. There is a constellation of equilibrium prices in the economy, facilitating the realization of models of capitalism. When the system reaches a state of disequilibrium as revealed in our case where a distribution of factor payments exhibits a disproportion, we may invoke what Immanuel Wallerstein called as a point of bifurcation (Wallerstein, 1999) like saying that the capitalist system has reached an inflection point, a turning point. From now on, the capitalism should reconsider its 'models of realization' to survive: 'The capitalist system has entered a terminal crisis:[10]

> Prigogine maintains that physical reality is for the most part characterized by non-equilibrium processes, in which order exists for a while, but then there inevitably occurs a point of 'bifurcation', in which two directions are equally possible. Furthermore, there is indeterminacy in physical reality, for it cannot be known in advance which option will be taken.[11]

Invoking this kind of 'non-equilibrium processes' (Prigogine) within the physical reality, along with our perceived states of disequilibrium within the monetarist perspective of the economy, lead us towards considering the points of 'bifurcation' as being moments when a certain system manifests two equally possible directions. The main challenge in the economy is that the equal likelihood is annulled through consequences of processes as in fractional reserve banking. The mechanism of debt creation mediated by the multiplying effect of the money in the economy facilitates the unique manifestation of the bifurcation in the economic reality, whereas such moments allows for two equally possible directions in the physical reality as evidenced by Prigogine.

---

10   Charles McKelvey http://www.globallearning-cuba.com/umlthe-view-from-the-southuml/the-terminal-crisis-of-the-world-system, retrieved on 07.04.2015

11   Cf. Prigagone (1997), citing Immanuel Wallerstein, *The terminal Crisis of the World-System.*

The point of 'bifurcation' might be regarded as 'inflection point',[12] a moment from which a system, an economy, industry, sector or a geopolitical situation, a significant turning point or factor of differentiation along the historical evolution of capitalism is taking place.

From the Third to the Fourth Capitalism: The core competence's differentiator of capitalism

ANY INITIATIVE, ANY ACTION FROM WORKS OF MERCY TO ACTS OF TRADE, is successful only if such actions complement co-existing unique resources, which are inferentially testified by a certain social actor's capability of harmonizing different species of capital. Therefore, such a type of unique resource is but indirectly confirmed through the difference that can be determined between two entrepreneurs owning, for instance, the same initial capital but with only one becoming successful. What would be the rationale behind such facts? The answer would be that such immeasurable parameter called 'co- existing unique resource' or 'alpha'-type quasi-rent (conventionally called as such) came into play. The competitive value of the business declines and the 'power' of added value decreases to zero when the *co-existent unique resource* vanishes. Therefore, we may depict the rise and fall of great civilizations (as well as states, eras, etc.) as being based on such a quasi-rent factor.

Hamel and Prahalad (1990) are the originators of the concept of core competence, in their famous treaty called *The Core Competence of the Corporation*, which paved the way toward the awareness of such unique resources. These type of unique resources made the distinction between an organization employing non-distinctive factors of production and another being able to deploy resources in a way that would differentiate that business from its competitors. *The applicability of the concept of core*

---

12   'An event that results in a significant change in the progress of a company, industry, sector, economy or geopolitical situation. An inflection point can be considered a turning point after which a dramatic change, with either positive or negative results, is expected to result. Companies, industries, sectors and economies are dynamic and constantly evolving. Inflection points are more significant than the small day-to-day progress that is made and the effects of the change are often well- known and widespread.' (Investopedia)

competence makes the distinction between the functionalist justification of the organization and the idea (a new economic philosophy) that each enterprise should create for itself a distinctive pattern and maintain it in order to become successfully. This new economic philosophy is like a personalist perspective upon the corporation and/or a certain business space varying in size (dimensionally).

Capitalism proved to be successful based on creating factors of differentiation along its historic evolution. One of the recent factors of success during the last cyclical phase of the modern world system could be explained through the lens of functionalism in the science of management. Later, Hamel and Prahalad highlighted a new critical success factor that might have been responsible with activating the post-modern phase of our world capitalist system – this new factor being the *core competence's differentiator*. This new phase of development is, actually, responsible for the affirmation of the so-called '*third capitalism*' and now we can observe the fatigue of this capitalism, by contemplating the causes and consequences of the last major capitalist crisis that rocked the world in 2008. The amplitude of this crisis is just a confirmation of the demise of a capitalist system developed since its major inception at the beginning of the 20th Century. Another major world economic crisis (The Great Depression) triggered major changes of the capitalist system that, ironically, found its ally in WW2 when governments of powerful states (the US, for instance) spent enormous amount of money on arming the Allied forces. The government expenditures might be regarded as having a function similar to a fuel boost pump. The U.S. government spent enormously to arm the Allied armed forces.[13] Stimulating the aggregate demand through an enormous spiral of spending on supplying the Allied armed forces with military equipment and ammunition has metamorphosed into an economic engine of producing and supplying goods and services during peacetime. The transition from a centralized bureaucratized US economic machine of supplying what

---

13   'In 1944, government spending at all levels accounted for 55% of gross domestic product (GDP). By 1947, government spending had dropped 75% in real terms, or from 55% of GDP to just over 16% of GDP.' (David R. Henderson, "U.S. Post-War Miracle" (working paper, Mercatus Center at George Mason University, 2010).

needed during the war to a free economic system capable of finding its point of equilibrium proved to be a real miracle of the US economy. The US economy was centralized[14] during wartime and, after the end of the WW2 the same economic system released from its centralized command function was capable to find its equilibrium in a very short time.[15]

World War II was, above all, a burst of deficit-financed government spending...[that] created an economic boom... [which] laid the foundation for long-run prosperity.[16]

This is the essence of the Second Capitalism that emerged from a world of the Great Depression and from the levelling functionalism of an economic system that proved to be successful as evidenced in the case of the US economy. The Keynes' doctrine became the proper justification and, consequently, the main economic discourse of the proponents of the Second Capitalism's system.

Capitalism subsists historically only if it has the capability to create factors of its internal differentiation. In default of such a creative power, capitalism fails. Basically, such a failure does not affect the system itself, but its evolutionary form (formation). This is the reason for the evolutionary

---

14   'An array of federal bureaucracies, including the Office of Price Administration, the War Production Board, the Office of Civilian Requirements, and War Manpower Commission directed resource allocation to arm and equip the millions of American and Allied soldiers in battle against the Axis enemy.' (Cecil Bohanon, 2012) Source: http://mercatus.org/publication/economic-recovery-lessons-post-world-war-ii-period

15   'In 1944, government spending at all levels accounted for 55% of gross domestic product (GDP). By 1947, government spending had dropped 75% in real terms, or from 55% of GDP to just over 16% of GDP.' [David R. Henderson, "U.S. Post-War Miracle" (working paper, Mercatus Center at George Mason University, 2010).] Over roughly the same period, federal tax revenues fell by only around 11%. ["National Income and Product Accounts Tables, 1940–1947" (GDP accounts in billions of chained 1937 dollars), Bureau of Economic Analysis, U.S. Department of Commerce, http://bea.gov/iTable. cfm?ReqID=9&step=1.] Yet this "destimulation" did not result in a collapse of consumption spending or private investment. Real consumption rose by 22% between 1944 and 1947 and spending on durable goods more than doubled in real terms. Gross private investment rose by 223% in real terms, with a whopping six-fold real increase in residential-housing expenditures. [Henderson, "U.S. Post-War Miracle."]

16   Paul Krugman, "1938 in 2010," *New York Times*, September 5, 2010.

approach of capitalism. Our applied study refers mainly to the coming of the fourth capitalism. To enlighten such an issue is equivalent to shedding light on the rise and decline of each historical type of capitalism. Having investigated the rise and fall of historical capitalism, my conclusion is that there are four types of historical capitalisms and that humanity has already entered the age of the fourth capitalism. Capitalism proved to be hegemonic through its differentiated evolution, enabled by factors of competitive and often conflicting dynamicities. Hence it gives support to regional conflicting capitalisms or is taken over within a new historical type of capitalism. As a matter of fact, each type of historical capitalism has contributed to filtering *patterns of capitalism* that can be perpetuated as *paradigmatic formulas of capitalist reproduction*.

The evolution of historical capitalisms has the same formula with the 'convergence-divergence cycle' of knowledge in science and technology. In our analysis we have come to a *tetradic model* for the historical cycle of the evolution of capitalism. Each one of the four types of historical capitalism are based on a four-part structure. This four-part structure has internally structured double complementary processing schemes: a convergence scheme is followed by a divergence scheme exactly like in the 'convergence-divergence cycle' of knowledge in science and technology, as already mentioned. The convergence phase includes two symmetrical sequences or sub-phases: a creative sub-phase (A) 'dominated by synergism between components of the system', confirmed by the strength of dominant economic paradigm, and a sub-phase (B) dominated by 'integration and/or fusion of the components into a new system'. Both are followed by a 'divergence phase' (CD) with an innovation sub-phase (C), 'leading to new competences and products', and an 'outcome sub-phase (D) consisting of new application and new inputs into the creative phases A of successive cycles' (Roco et al., 2013, p. 13). As I have already mentioned, I have documented in my own research a convergence- divergence type of process (similar with the one envisioned by Roco et al) for the field of historical capitalisms, more precisely for the evolution of the paradigms of historical capitalism.[17] The levelling functionalism of classical paradigms

---

17   The same type of "knowledge confluence spiral" (Roco et al., 2013) can be

in economics, proper to the first historical capitalism, was dominated by the synergism between European national schools of economic thought determined by the authority of A. Smith and D. Ricardo's theories and doctrine (everybody used to think in Ricardo's way of thinking or in a Smith-ian way of thinking). An innovative sub-phase (C) followed this convergence phase (AB), being dominated by the affirmation of List-ian theory and doctrine proper to the second historical capitalism. *This type of capitalism was leading to new competences and products and to a new way of thinking illustrated by the paradigm of corporatism.* The outcome phase (D) of this evolutionary sequence resulted in new application and inputs into the creative (A) phases of the successive cycles of historical 'confluence spiral'. There were some attempts to assemble such interacting parts of the worlds of historical capitalisms by advancing on the path of typologizing them. Nevertheless, there are still missing pieces of the complex puzzle of historical capitalisms and several key thinkers have started to solve this puzzle. Our own analysis aims for the same purposive challenging goal. We may detect that the fourth capitalism is properly a capitalism of convergence being that the outcome of the third capitalism phase represents the inputs into a new creative phase, re-opening the historical spiral. Basically speaking, this convergence appears to be not any more like a bald, merely horizontal one but rather like an enlarged and vertical one so that we may call it meta-convergence.

Combining the hypothesis of the fourth capitalism with the idea of convergence clarifies the mechanism of the evolution of universal capitalism in four stages (the four stages are somehow equivalent to the four types of historical capitalism). The last capitalism has many trans-historical elements and therefore, a universalist vocation. Such trans-historical elements are, for instance: unique inimitable resources and, therefore, immeasurable, the meta-convergence with revealed doxology – as in the example of the Christian ethos of Northern capitalists – textbook pedagogy of natural systems (the idea that optimal utilizations are stored in any kind of thing through a sort of latent levelling boards, never exhausted in concrete manifestations of that kind of thing). Finally, thinking on the

---

documented in the field of evolutionary paradigms of historical capitalism.

fourth capitalism as the capitalism of convergence we detected the fourfold model of generic, universal capitalism. However, I need to underline the idea that capitalism can go on towards a luminous plateau, equivalent with a human capitalism wherein the universal law of meta-convergence will govern along the tendency to bring into harmony the quest for profit with the quest for welfare.

References

Abrahamson, P. (1999): 'The Welfare Modelling Business', in *Social Policy and Administration* 33 (4): 394-415

Adascalitei, D. (2012): Welfare State Development in Central and Eastern Europe: A State of the Art Literature Review. In: *Studies of Transition States and Societies*, 4, issue 2, p. 59-70

Aidukaite, J. (2009): Old welfare state theories and new welfare regimes in Eastern Europe: Challenges and implications. In: *Communist and Post-Communist Studies* 42(1): 23-39

Aidukaite, J. (2011): Welfare reforms and socio-economic trends in the 10 new EU member states of Central and Eastern Europe. In: *Communist and Post-Communist Studies* 44(3): 211–219

Alcock, P., Powell, M. (2010) (eds.): Welfare Theory and Development, SAGE Library of Health and Social Welfare

Aman, Alfred C. Jr., (1998): The Globalizing State: A Future-Oriented Perspective on the Public/Private Distinction, Federalism, and Democracy, *Vanderbilt Journal of Transnational Law* 31(4): 769, 870

Anderson, K. M. (2001): The Politics of Retrenchment in a Social Democratic Welfare State: Reform of Swedish Pensions and Unemployment Insurance. *Comparative Political Studies*, 34(9), 1063–1091

Appadurai, A. (1996). *Modernity at Large*. Minneapolis: University of Minnesota Press

Arcanjo, M. (2006) "Ideal (and Real) types of welfare state", ISEG/UTL, Department of Economics, WP06. http://econpapers.repec.org/paper/iseisegwp/wp62006.htm]

Arts, W., Gelissen, J. (2002) Three worlds of welfare capitalism or more? *Journal of European Social Policy* 12 (2): 137-158

Arts, Wil; Gelissen, J. (2010) Models of the Welfare State. In: Castles, F. G. et al. *The Oxford Handbook of the Welfare State*. Oxford: Oxford University Press

Aspalter, C. (2006). New Developments in the Theory of Comparative Social Policy in *Journal of Comparative Social Welfare* 22(1): 3-22

Aspalter, C. (2009). The development of ideal-typical welfare regime theory. In: *International Social Work*. Nov. 2011, vol. 54, no. 6, 735-750

Aspalter, C., K. Jinsoo and P. Sojeung (2009). Analysing the Welfare State in Poland, the Czech Republic, Hungary and Slovenia: An Ideal-Typical Perspective. *Social Policy and Administration* 43(2): 170-185

Aspalter, Christiansen (2011). The development of ideal-typical welfare regime theory. *International Social Work*, 54(6) 735–750

Avlijas, S. (2014). Capitalist Diversity on Europe's Periphery. Zagreb, The Institute of Economics, Zagreb. 16: 147-159

Avram, S., H. Levy and Sutherland, H. (2014). Income redistribution in the European Union. IZA J Labor Stud 3(1): 1-29

Badescu, C. and Badescu, I. (2014). *Conversiunea sistemelor. Pustiul postmodern si deformarea lumii. Probleme epistemologice ale teoriei conversiunii sistemelor* (Systems' Conversion. Postmodern Solitude and the World Distortion. Epistemological Problems on the Theory of Systems' Conversion). Mica Valahie Press

Badescu, C. (2013). *Fundamentele culturale ale crizelor economice De la etnoeconomie la teoria proprietății identitare* (Cultural Foundations of Economic Crises From Ethnoeconomy to the Theory of Identitary Property), Ed. Muzeului Național al Literaturii Române, București

Badescu, C. (2013). Some Considerations on a New Typology of Welfare Regimes, in Zamfir, E; Maggino, F. (eds.), *The European Culture for Human Rights: The Right to Happiness*, Cambridge Scholars Publishing, pp. 356-367

Badescu, I.C., (2007). *Vertical Boundaries of the Firm: A Strategic Approach.* Mica Valahie Press

Badescu, I. (2008). *Tratat de geopolitica, (Treatise on Geopolitics)*, Mica Valahie Press

Badescu, I. (2009). Despre criza in lumina teoriei succesiunii coexistente (About Crisis in the Light of the Theory of Coexistent Succession), Bucuresti: Editura Centrului de Informare si Documentare Economica

Badescu, I. (2013). *Noology. On the Spiritual Order of the World. The System of Noological Sociology.* Romanian Academy

Badescu, I. (2011). [online] *Migratia romanilor in Italia (Romanian Migrants in Italy)*, www.Sociologiaazi.ro [August 2014]

Badescu, I., Cucu-Oancea, O. (2011). *Dictionar de sociologie rurala* (Dictionary of Rural Sociology). Bucuresti: Mica Valahie Press

Bakewell, Oliver (2011). Migration and Development in sub-Saharan Africa. In: *International Political Economy* Yearbook, 17, 136-158

Baldock, J. et al. (eds.) (2012). *Social Policy*, 4th ed. Oxford: Oxford University Press Bambra, C. (2004a). Weathering the Storm: Convergence, Divergence and the Robustness of the "Worlds of Welfare". *The Social Policy Journal* 3(3): 3-23

Bambra, C. (2004b). The worlds of welfare: illusory and gender blind? *Social Policy and Society*, 3 (3). pp. 201-212

Bambra, C. (2005) 'Worlds of welfare and the health care discrepancy.', Social policy and society., 4 (1). pp. 31-41

Bambra, C. (2006a). Decommodification and the worlds of welfare revisited. *Journal of European social policy* 16(1): 73-80

Bambra, C. (2006b). Health Status and the Worlds of Welfare. *Social Policy and Society* 5(1): 53-62

Bambra, C. (2007). Going beyond The three worlds of welfare capitalism: regime theory and public health research. In: *Journal of Epidemiology & Community Health* 61(12): 1098-1102

Bambra, C. and T. A. Eikemo (2009). Welfare state regimes, unemployment and health: a comparative study of the relationship between unemployment and self- reported health in 23 European countries. *Journal of epidemiology and community health* 63(2): 92

Barrientos, A. (2015). A Veritable Mountain of Data and Years of Endless Statistical Manipulation: Methods in the Three Worlds and After. *Social Policy and Society*, 14(2), 259-270

Barr, N. A. (1993). *The Economics of the Welfare State*, New York: Oxford University Press

Bastia, T. (Ed.) (2013). *Migration and Inequality*, Routledge

Beck, U. (1992). *Risk Society. Towards a New Modernity*, London: Sage Publications. Berg-Schlosser, D., DeMeur, G. (1994). Conditions of democracy in interwar Europe: a Boolean test of major hypotheses. *Comparative Politics* 26 (3), 253-279

Blau, J. (1989). Theories of the Welfare State, *Social Service Review*, Vol. 63, No. 1, pp. 26-38

Block, F. (2001) Introduction. In: Polanyi, K. (2001). *The Great Transformation The Political and Economic Origins of Our Time*. Boston: Beacon Press

Bohle, D. (2007). The State, Internationalization, and Capitalist Diversity in Eastern Europe. *Competition & Change* 11(2): 89-116

Boisot, M., & MacMillan, I. (2004). Crossing Epistemological Boundaries: Managerial and Entrepreneurial Approaches to Knowledge Management. Long Range Planning, 37 (6), 505-524. http://dx.doi.org/10.1016/j.lrp.2004.09.002

Bonilla, F. et al. (eds.) (1998). *Borderless Borders: US Latinos, Latins Americans, and the Paradox of Interdependence*, Philadelphia: Temple University Press

Bonoli, G. 1997. Classifying Welfare States: a Two Dimensional Approach. *Journal of Social Policy* 26(3):351-372

Bonoli, G. et al. (2000). *European welfare futures*. Cambridge: Polity Press.

Brenner, N. (1998). Global cities, glocal states: Global city formation and state territorial restructuring in contemporary Europe, *Review of International Political Economy*, 5 (2): 1–37

Briggs, A. (1961). "The Welfare State in Historical Perspective." European Journal of Sociology 2(2): 221-258

Brockhoff, S. et al. (2012). The three worlds of welfare capitalism revisited. IDEAS Working Paper Series from RePEc

Buhr, D. and Stoy, V. (2015). More than just Welfare Transfers? A Review of the Scope of Esping-Andersen's Welfare Regime Typology. *Social Policy and Society* 14(2): 271- 285

Byrne, J; Humble, A. M., (2006). An Introduction to Mixed Method Research. Atlantic Research Centre for Family-Work Issues, Mount Saint Vincent University Business for Social Responsibility (2008). International Labor Migration: A Responsible Role for Business, https://www.bsr.org/reports/BSR_LaborMigrationRoleforBusiness. Pdf [accessed 28.10.2019]

Cameron, D.R. (1984). Social democracy, corporatism, labour quiescence and the representation of economic interest in advanced capitalism.

In: Goldthorpe, John H. (Ed.), *Order and Conflict in Contemporary Capitalism: Studies in the Political Economy of Western European Nations*, Conference Papers. Clarendon, Oxford, pp. 143-178

Carter, B. & Rohwerder, B. (2016). Rapid fragility and migration assessment for Ethiopia (Rapid Literature Review). Birmingham, UK: GSDRC, University of Birmingham. Castles, F. (1998). *Comparative Public Policy. Patterns of Postwar Transformation*, Cheltenham: Edward Elgar

Castles, F. and H. Obinger (2008). Worlds, Families, Regimes: Country Clusters in European and OECD Area Public Policy. *West European Politics* 31(1-2): 321-344

Central Statistical Agency (2013). *Population Projections for Ethiopia 2007-2037*, Addis Ababa

Cerami, A. (2006). *Social Policy in Central and Eastern Europe: The Emergence of a New European Welfare Regime*. Berlin: Lit Verlag

Cerami, A., Vanhuysse (eds.) 2009. *Post-Communist Welfare Pathways: Theorizing Social Policy Transformations in Central and Eastern Europe*. London: Palgrave Macmillan

Cousins, M. (2005). *European Welfare States: Comparative Perspectives*. London: SAGE Publications Ltd

Danforth (2010): *The Emergence of Three Worlds of Welfare*, PhD paper

Danforth, B. (2014). Worlds of welfare in time: A historical reassessment of the three- world typology. *Journal of European Social Policy* 24(2): 164-182

Deacon, B., (1992a). East European welfare: Past, present and future in comparative context. In: B. Deacon (ed.) *The New Eastern Europe – Social Policy Past, Present and Future*. London: Sage, ch.1

Deacon, B., (1992b). The future of social policy in Eastern Europe, in B. Deacon, (ed.), *The New Eastern Europe: Social Policy Past, Present and Future*. Sage Publications, London, pp. 167-192

Deacon, B. (1993). Developments in East European social policy. In: *New Perspectives on the Welfare State in Europe*, edited by C. Jones. London: Routledge

Deacon, B. (1995). Global Social Policy Actors and the Shaping of East European Welfare. *International Journal of Sociology* 25(1): 40-80

Deacon, B., (1997). International organizations and the making of post-Communist social policy. In: Deacon, Bob, Hulse, Michelle, Stubbs, Paul (Eds.), *Global Social Policy International Organizations and the Future of Welfare*. Sage Publications, London, pp. 91-153

Deacon, B. (2000). Eastern European welfare states: the impact of the politics of globalization. *Journal of European Social Policy* 10 (2):146-161

Deakin, N. et al. (eds.) (2004). Welfare and The State Critical Concepts in Political Science. Volume IV *Welfare Futures*, Abingdon: Routledge

Draxler, Juraj and van Vliet, Olaf, European Social Model: No Convergence from the East (January 15, 2010). Journal of European Integration, Vol. 32, No. 1, pp. 115-135, 2010. Available at SSRN: https://ssrn.com/abstract=1538184

Ebbinghaus, B. & Manow, P. (eds.) (2001). *Comparing welfare capitalism*. London: Routledge

Ebbinghaus, B. (1998). Europe through the Looking-Glass: Comparative and Multi- Level Perspectives. *Acta Sociologica* 41(4): 301-313

Ebbinghaus, B. (2015). *Welfare Retrenchment*: 521-527

Ebbinghaus, B., M. A. Orenstein and N. Whiteside (2012). Shifting responsibilities in Western European pension systems: What future for social models? *Global Social Policy* 12(3): 266-282

Ebbinghaus, B. (2012). Comparing Welfare State Regimes: Are Typologies an Ideal or Realistic Strategy? ESPAnet Conference, Edinburgh, September 6-8

Esping-Andersen, G. (1990). *The Three Worlds of Welfare Capitalism*. Cambridge: Polity Press & Princeton: Princeton University Press

Esping-Andersen, G. (1996). After the Golden Age: The Future of the Welfare State in the New World Order. *Desarrollo Economico* 36(142): 523-554

Esping-Andersen, G. (1999). *New Social Risks in Old Welfare States*, Oxford: Oxford University Press

Esping-Andersen, G. (2013). *The Three Worlds of Welfare Capitalism* [electronic resource]. Oxford: Wiley

Esping-Andersen, G. (1999). *Social Foundation of Postindustrial Economies*. Oxford: Oxford University Press

Esping-Andersen, G. (ed.) (1996). *Welfare States in Transition: National Adaptations in Global Economies*. London: SAGE

Esping-Andersen, G. (1994). Welfare states and the economy. In: Smelser, Neil J., Swedberg, Richard (Eds.) *The Handbook of Economic Sociology*. Princeton University Press, Princeton, NJ, pp. 691-711

Farkas, B. (2011). The Central and Eastern European model of capitalism. *Post- Communist Economies* 23(1): 15-35

Fenger, H.J.M. (2007). Welfare regimes in Central and Eastern Europe: Incorporating post-communist countries in a welfare regime typology. In: *Contemporary Issues and Ideas in Social Sciences*, 3(2): 1- 30

Ferge, Z. (1997). "The Changed Welfare Paradigm: The Individualization of The Social." Social Policy & Administration 31(1): 20-44

Ferge, Z. (2001). Welfare and 'Ill-fare' Systems in Central-Eastern Europe. In Globalization and European Welfare States: Challenges and Change, edited by B. Sykes, B. Palier and M. Prior. Basingstoke: Palgrave

Ferge, Z. and J. E. Kolberg (1992). Social policy in a changing Europe / Zsuzsa Ferge, Jon Eivind Kolberg, eds. Frankfurt am Main: Boulder, Colo., Campus Verlag; Westview Press

Ferragina, E., M. Seeleib-Kaiser and T. Spreckelsen (2015). "The Four Worlds of 'Welfare Reality'- Social Risks and Outcomes in Europe" Social Policy and Society 14(2): 287-307

Ferragina, E.; Seeleib-Kaiser, Martin (2011). Thematic Review: Welfare regime debate: past, present, futures? In: Policy and Politics 39(4): 583-611(29)

Ferreira, L.V. and Figueiredo, A. (2005), "Welfare Regimes in the EU 15 and in the Enlarged Europe: An exploratory analysis", FEP, WP No. 176

Filandri, M. and M. Olagnero (2014). „Housing Inequality and Social Class in Europe." Housing Studies 29(7): 977-993

Flora, P. (a cura di), *Growth to Limits. The Western European Welfare States Since World War II*, Berlino — New York, Walter de Gruyter, Volume I: *Sweden, Norway, Finland, Denmark*, 1986, pp. XXXVI-381,

DM 158; Volume II: *Germany, United Kingdom, Ireland, Italy*, 1986, pp. XXXVI-499, DM 202; Volume IV: *Appendix (Synopses, Bibliographies, Tables)*, 1987, pp. X-337, DM 200

Food and Agriculture Organization of the United Nations (2017). *Evidence on internal and international migration patterns in selected African countries* FAO's Statistics Division and Social Policies and Rural Institutions Division

Friedland, R., Alford, R.R. 1991. Bringing Society Back in: Symbols, Practices, and Institutional Contradictions. pp. 232–266 in The New Institutionalism in Organizational Analysis, edited by Walter W. Powell and Paul J. DiMaggio. Chicago: University of Chicago Press

Frigg, R. and Hartmann, S. (2018). "Models in Science", *The Stanford Encyclopedia of Philosophy* (Summer 2018 Edition), Edward N. Zalta (ed.), URL = <https://plato. stanford.edu/archives/sum2018/entries/models-science/>

Fuchs, S.; Offe, C. (2008). Welfare State Formation in the Enlarged European Union Patterns of Reform in the Post-Communist New Member States. Hertie School of Governance – working papers, No. 14

Georgescu-Roegen, Nicholas (1971). The Entropy Law and the Economic Process. Harvard University Press

Giddens, A. (1984) The Constitution of Society. Outline of the Theory of Structuration. Cambridge: Polity

Goedemé, T. 2009. [Review of the book 'Welfare States in East Central Europe, 1919– 2004' by Tomasz Inglot], Sociologický časopis/Czech Sociological Review, Vol. 45, No. 6

Gough, I. (2001). Social assistance regimes: a cluster analysis. In: Journal of European social policy, 11 (2): 165-170

Gough, I. (2003). European social policy lessons: 12 theses. In: Marshall, K. and Butzbach, O., (eds.) New social policy agendas for Europe and Asia - challenges, experience, and lessons. The World Bank, Washington DC, USA, pp. 15-2

Gough, I. (2008). European welfare states: explanations and lessons for developing countries. In: Dani, Anis Ahmad and Haan, Harjan de, (eds.) Inclusive states: social policy and structural inequalities. World

Bank Publications, Washington, USA, pp. 3-38

Gough, I. (2010). Economic crisis, climate change and the future of welfare states. 21st Century society, 5 (1): 51-64

Gough, I.; Wood, G. (2004). Conclusion: rethinking social policy in development contexts. In: Insecurity and welfare regimes in Asia, Africa and Latin America. Cambridge University Press, Cambridge, UK, pp. 312-326

Gumilev L. N. 1978–1979. Ethnogenesis and Earth's Biosphere. Lubertsy, Moscow. In Russian (Гумилев Л. Н. Этногенез и биосфера Земли. Люберцы, Москва). Полное или частичное копирование материалов сайта www.sociostudies.org разрешено только при обязательном указании автора и прямой гиперссылки

Hacker, B. (2009). Hybridization instead of Clustering: Transformation Processes of Welfare Policies in Central and Eastern Europe. In: Social Policy and Administration 43(2): 152-169

Haggard, S., & Kaufman, R. R. (2008). Development, Democracy, and Welfare States: Latin America, East Asia, and Eastern Europe. Princeton, NJ: Princeton University Press

Hanusch, H., Wackermannn, F. 2009. Global Financial Crisis: Causes and Lessons A Neo-Schumpeterian perspective, Beitrag Nr. 303, Volkswirtchaftliche Diskussionsreihe

Hassan, Seid Y. and Negash, Minga (2013). *Explaining the Ethiopian Outmigration: Incentives or Constraints?*

Hausermann, S. (2006). Changing Coalitions in Social Policy Reforms: The Politics of New Social Needs and Demands. In: Journal of European Social Policy 16(1): 5-21 Hellman, J. S., Jones, G., Kaufmann, D. (2000). Seize the State, Seixe the Day: State Capture, Corruption, and Influence in Transition. Policy Research Working Paper. The World Bank

Hicks, A., Misra, J., Nang Ng, T., 1995. The programmatic emergence of the social security state. American Sociological Review 60 (3), 329-349. http://www.hertieschool.org/fileadmin/images/Downloads/working_papers/14.pdf

Hignet, K. (2012). Power and Privilege: Elite Lifestyles in Communist Eastern Europe. Source: https://thevieweast.wordpress.com/2012/

04/23/power-and-privilege-in-communist-eastern-europe/ (accessed 05.08.2019)

Higgott, Richard (2016). 'Regional Worlds, Regional Institutions: Towards the Regional Economic Institutionalisation of East Asia?', CSGR Working Paper No. 280/16, Centre for the Study of Globalisation and Regionalisation, University of Warwick. Available at: www.warwick. ac.uk/csgr/papers/280-16.pdf (accessed 06.09.2019)

Hirschman, A, O. (1994). *The Rise and Decline of Development Economics* In: Kanth, R. (ed.) *Paradigms in Economic Development: Classic Perspectives, Critiques, and Reflections*, New York: M. E. Sharpe

Hirschman, A, O. (2013). The Essential Hirschman. Princeton, NJ: Princeton University Press

Huber, E., Stephens, J.D., 1996. Internationalisation and the social democratic model: crisis and future prospects. In: Paper Delivered at the Third Peder Sarher Symposium: Challenges to Labour: Integration, Employment, and Bargaining in Scandinavia and United States, Berkeley, CA, 21-22 March, First Half.

Hudson, J. R., & Kühner, S. (2012). Analyzing the Productiveand Protective Dimensions of Welfare: Looking Beyond the OECD. *Social Policy and Administration*, 46(1), 35- 60. DOI: 10.1111/j.1467-9515.2011.00813.x

Huo, J. et al. (2008). Decommodification and activation in social democratic policy: resolving the paradox. In: Journal of European Social Policy, 18(1)

Inglot, T. (2008). Welfare States in East Central Europe, 1919–2004. Cambridge: Cambridge University Press

Inglot, T. (2008). Introduction: Understanding Past and Present Social Policy Development in East Central Europe. Cambridge, Cambridge: Cambridge University Press

Inglot, T. (2013). "Western welfare states watched from the East during the Cold War: condemnation, competition, and creative learning." Journal of International and Comparative Social Policy 29(3): 241-257

Inglot, T. and T. Goedemé (2009). Welfare states in East Central Europe, 1919-2004. T. Inglot and T. Goedemé. 45: 1316-1317

International Organization for Migration (2018). *Global Migration Indicators*, Source: www.migrationdataportal.org

Jakab, Zoltán and Kumhof, Michael, (2015), Banks are not intermediaries of loanable funds – and why this matter, No 529, Bank of England working papers, Bank of England, https://EconPapers.repec.org/RePEc:boe:boeewp:0529

Joel S Hellman, J. S., et al. (2003). Seize the state, seize the day: state capture and influence in transition economies, Journal of Comparative Economics, Volume 31, Issue 4, Pages 751-773, https://doi.org/10.1016/j.jce.2003.09.006

Johansson, H., Panican, A. (2016). Combating Poverty in Local Welfare Systems London: Palgrave Macmillan

Jonas, Andrew, 1994. The Scale Politics of Spatiality, Environment and Planning D, *Society and Space*, 12(3): 257–64

Joyce, M., Lasaosa, A., Stevens, I., & Tong, M. (2010). The financial market impact of quantitative easing. Bank of England Working Paper, 393

Kasza, G. (2002). 'The illusion of welfare regimes', Journal of Social Policy, 31, 2, 271– 287

Kaufman, Robert R. (2007). Market Reform and Social Protection: Lessons from the Czech Republic, Hungary, and Poland. In: East European Politics & Societies, 21: 111- 125

Kennett, P. (Ed.) (2013). A Handbook of Comparative Social Policy, Second Edition. Cheltenham: Edward Elgar

Keynes, J. M. (2007). The General Theory of Employment, Interest and Money. London: Macmillan

Kim, Ki-tae. (2015). "From Worlds to Cases: Case Selection and 'Other Worlds' in the Welfare Modelling Business." Social Policy and Society 14(2): 309-321

Kitschelt, H., 1999. European social democracy between political economy and electoral competition. In: Kitschelt, Herbert, et al. (Eds.), Continuity and Change in Contemporary Capitalism. Cambridge University Press, Cambridge, pp. 1-37

Klenner, C. and Leiber, S. (eds.) (2010) Welfare States and Gender Inequality in Central and Eastern Europe. Continuity and Post-Socialist Transformation in EU- Member States, Wiesbaden-VS Verlag

Kluge, Susann (2000). Empirically Grounded Construction of Types and Typologies in Qualitative Social Research [14 paragraphs]. *Forum Qualitative Sozialforschung / Forum: Qualitative Social Research*, 1(1), Art. 14, http://nbn-resolving.de/urn:nbn: de:0114-fqs0001145

Kominek, J. (2009). Each institutionalization elementary is a self-reinforcing process increasing path dependency, University of Hamburg, Research Group Climate Change and Security, working Paper CLISEC-4

Korkut, U. (2009). [Review of the book "Welfare States in East Central Europe 1919–2004 by Thomasz, Inglot]. Journal of European Social Policy, July 2009 19: 283 Korkut, U. (2008). Social Policy in Central and Eastern Europe: The Emergence of a New European Welfare Regime. U. Korkut and A. Cerami. 44: 595-597

Kornai, J. (1992). The Socialist System: The Political Economy of Communism. Princeton, NJ: Princeton

Korpi, W., & Palme, J. (1998). The Paradox of Redistribution and Strategies of Equality: Welfare State Institutions, Inequality, and Poverty in the Western Countries. *American Sociological Review*, 63(5), 661-687. Retrieved from http://www.jstor.org/stable/2657333

Kuitto, K. (2011). More than just money: Patterns of disaggregated welfare expenditure in the enlarged Europe. In: Journal of European Social Policy, Oct. 2011 vol 21 no. 348- 364

Kuitto, K. (2016). Post-communist welfare states in European context. Cheltenham: Edward Elgar Publishing

Kureková, L. (2013). "Welfare Systems as Emigration Factor: Evidence from the New Accession States Welfare Systems as Emigration Factor: Evidence from the New Accession States." Journal of Common Market Studies 51(4): 721-739

Korpi, W., 1983. The Democratic Class Struggle. Routledge & Kegan Poul, London

Lampert, J. (2006). Deleuze and Guattari's Philosophy of History, London: Continuum

Landman, T. 2003. Issues and Methods in Comparative Politics: An Introduction, 3rd Ed., Abingdon: Routledge

Lee, S. M., Olson, D. L. (2010). Convergenomics: Strategic Innovation in the Convergence Era, Gower Publishing

Lehmbruch, G., 1984. Concentration and the structure of corporatist networks. In: Goldthorpe, John H. (Ed.), Order and Conflict in Contemporary Capitalism. Clarendon Press, Oxford, pp. 60-80

Leibrecht, M; Klien, M; Onaran, Ö (2011). Globalization, welfare regimes and social protection expenditures in Western and Eastern European countries

Lendvai, N. (2008). EU Integration and the Transformation of Post-communist Welfare: Traversing a 'Quantum Leap'? In: Social Policy & Administration, 42(5): 504-523

Levy, J. D. (2010). Welfare Retrenchment. In: Castles, F. G. et al. (Eds.) The Oxford Handbook of the Welfare State. Oxford: Oxford University Press

Lofgren, Mike, *Anatomy of the Deep State*, Retrieved from: (http://billmoyers.com/2014/02/21/anatomy-of-the-deep-state/) [21.02.2014]

Lodemel, I. (1989). *The quest for institutional welfare and the problem of the residuum: the case of income maintenance and personal social care policies in Norway and Britain 1946 to 1966*. PhD thesis, The London School of Economics and Political Science (LSE)

Lovejoy, S., A. F. Tuck, S. J. Hovde, and D. Schertzer (2007), Is isotropic turbulence relevant in the atmosphere? *Geophys. Res. Lett.*, 34, L15802, doi: 10.1029/ 2007GL029359

Lyonnet, V., Werner, R. (2012). Lessons from the Bank of England on 'quantitative easing' and other 'unconventional' monetary policies. International Review of Financial Analysis, 25:94-105

Maastricht Graduate School of Governance (2017). *Ethiopia Migration Profile: Study on Migration Routes in the East and Horn of Africa*

Maclean, M., Harvey, C. & Chia, R. (2012). Reflexive practice and the making of elite business careers. Management Learning, 43(4): 385-404

Marradi, A. (1990). Classification, typology, taxonomy. In: Quality & Quantity 24: 129-157

Massey, D. (1993). *Politics and Space/Time*, in M. Keith and S. Pile (eds) *Place and the Politics of Identity*, London and New York: Routledge, pp. 141–61

McLeay, M., Radia, A. and Thomas, R. (2014). Money creation in the modern economy, Quarterly Bulletin (Q1), Bank of England

Melnyk, J. (2008). *Victorian Religion: Faith and Life in Britain*. Westport, CT: Praeger

Myles, J., Quadagno, J. (2002). Political Theories of Welfare State. Social Service Review, March, http://citeseerx.ist.psu.edu/viewdoc/download ?doi=10.1.1.470.2094&rep=rep1& type=pdf)

Moore, M. (2004). The New Fiscal Sociology in Developing Countries, http://www. psa.ac.uk/cps/2004/moore.pdf

Moore, M. (2004). "Revenues, State Formation, and the Quality of Governance in Developing Countries". International Political Science Review/Revue internationale de science politique Vol. 25, No. 3, The Nation-State and Globalization: Changing Roles and Functions. Les États nations et la globalisation : Roles et fonctions en mutation (Jul., 2004), pp. 297-319

Motru, C. R. (1904). Cultura română și Politicianismul (Romanian culture and petty politics), Bucharest: Socec

OECD (2001). Agricultural Policies in OECD Countries: Monitoring and Evaluation 2000: Glossary of Agricultural Policy Terms, https://stats. oecd.org/glossary/detail.asp?ID=303

O'Connor, J. and G. Olsen (1998a). 'Introduction, Understanding the Welfare State: Power Resources Theory and Its Critics', in J. O'Connor and G. Olsen (eds) Power Resources Theory and the Welfare State: A Critical Appraisal. Essays Collected in Honor of Walter Korpi, Toronto: University of Toronto Press

O'Connor, J. and G. Olsen (eds) (1998b). Power Resources Theory and the Welfare State: A Critical Appraisal. Essays Collected in Honor of Walter Korpi, Toronto: University of Toronto Press

Orenstein, M. A. (2008). Postcommunist welfare states. In: Journal of Democracy, 19(4): 80-94

Papadopoulos, T., Roumpakis, A. (2013). Familistic welfare capitalism in crisis: social reproduction and anti-social policy in Greece - Journal of International and Comparative Social Policy, 2013

Philip Kitcher (2006), 'The Knowledge Business' in Erik J. Olsson (ed.), *Knowledge and Inquiry Essays on the Pragmatism of Isaac Levi*, Cambridge: Cambridge University Press, pp. 50-64

Pierson, P. (1996). The New Politics of the Welfare State. In: World Politics 48.2 (1996) 143-179

Pierson, P. (2000). Increasing Returns, Path Dependence, and the Study of Politics. The American Political Science Review, 94(2), 251-267. doi:10.2307/2586011

Pierson, P. (Ed.) (2001). The New Politics of the Welfare State. Oxford: Oxford Univ. Press

Pierson, P. (2009). The new politics of the welfare state. Oxford: Oxford Univ. Press Pierson, Christopher and Castles, Francis G. (2006). The welfare state reader (2nd ed.). Polity, Cambridge; Malden MA

Poder, K., Kerem, K. (2011). "Social Models" in a European Comparison: Convergence or Divergence? Eastern European economics, 49(5): 55–74

Polanec, S. (2004). Convergence at Last?: Evidence from Transition Countries. In: Eastern European Economics, Taylor & Francis Journals, vol. 42(4), pages 55-80, July

Pope, W. (1975). Durkheim as a Functionalist. The Sociological Quarterly, 16: 361– 379. doi: 10.1111/j.1533-8525.1975.tb00954.x

Postolache, T., (2007). Sur les «succesions coexistantes» au tournant des millenaires. Quelques reflexions epistemologiques, discurso de ingreso del Academico Correspondiente para Rumania, Real Academia de Ciencias Economicas y Financieras, Barcelona

Postolache, T., (2007). Vers un «ideal practicable». Notes et reflexions, Bucureşti, Editura Academiei Române

Pott, A., Rass, C., Wolff, F. (Eds.) (2018) Was ist ein Migrationregime? What Is a Migration Regime? Springer Fachmedien Wiesbaden

Powell, M. (2004) Welfare Regimes and the Welfare Mix (with A. Barrientos)', European Journal of Political Research, 43(1): 83-105

Powell, M. (2007). Understanding the Mixed Economy of Welfare (ed) Policy Press

Powell, M., Hewitt, M. (2002). Welfare State and Welfare Change, Open University Press: Buckingham

Powell, M., Kim, Ki-tae (2014). The "Chameleon" Korean Welfare Regime. In: Social Policy & Administration 48(6): 626-646

Powell, M. (2014). A Re-Specification of the Welfare State: Conceptual Issues in 'The Three Worlds of Welfare Capitalism. Social Policy and Society, doi:10.1017/ S1474746414000529

Powell, M.; Barrientos, A. (2011). An Audit of the Welfare Modelling Business. Social Policy & Administration, 45: 69–84

Powell, M. and A. Barrientos (2015). "Introduction: Twenty-Five Years of the Welfare Modelling Business." Social Policy and Society 14(2): 241-245

Prodnik, J. (2012). A Note on the Ongoing Processes of Commodification: From the Audience Commodity to the Social Factory, tripleC 10(2): 274-301, http://www.triple-c.at

Prahalad, C. K. and Hamel, Gary, The Core Competence of the Corporation (1990). Harvard Business Review, Vol. 68, Issue 3, p. 79-91 1990. Available at SSRN: https:// ssrn.com/abstract=1505251

Ratha, Dilip and Shaw, William (2007). *South-South Migration and Remittances.* World Bank Working Paper No. 102

Robert Wood Johnson Foundation, http://www.qualres.org/HomePosi-3515.html [07.03.2015]

Roco, M.C., Bainbridge, W.S., Tonn, B., Whitesides, G. (2014). Convergence of Knowledge, Technology, And Society: Beyond Convergence of Nano-Bio-Info- Cognitive Technologies, New York: Springer International Publishing Switzerland Rush, M. (2015). Between Two Worlds of Father Politics *USA or Sweden?* Manchester: Manchester University Press

Saint-Arnaud, S.; Bernard, P. (2003). Convergence or Resilience? A Hierarchical Cluster Analysis of the Welfare Regimes in Advanced Countries. In: Current Sociology 51(5): 499-527

Sanduleasa, Andra-Berta, (2014). [online] Gender, Status and Housework Inequality in Romania www.sociologiaazi.ro, nr 3 [Accessed in August 2014] Sassen, S. (1996). *Losing Control? Sovereignty in an Age of Globalization*, New York: Columbia University Press

Sassen, S. (2000a) Spatialities and Temporalities of the Global, *Public Culture*, 12(1) (Millenium Issue on Globalization. Re-issued by Duke University Press)

Sassen, S. (2000b). Territory and Territoriality in the Global Economy, *International Sociology*, 15(2): 372–93

Sassen, S. (2002). Towards a Sociology of Information Technology, *Current Sociology*. Special Issue on the New Information Technologies

Sassen, S. (2003). *Denationalization: Territory, Authority and Rights in a Global Digital Age.* (Under contract, Princeton, NJ: Princeton University Press)

Sassen, S. (2003). Globalization or Denationalization? *Review of International Political Economy, 10* (1), 1-22. http://www.jstor.org.manchester.idm.oclc.org/ stable/4177449

Sassen, S. (ed.) (2007). Deciphering the Global: Its Spaces, Scales and Subjects. London: Routledge

Sassen, S. (2010). The Global inside the national A research agenda for sociology", http://www.saskiasassen.com/PDFs/publications/the-global-inside-the-national.pdf [02/08/2018]

Sassen, S. (2012). 'Expanding the Terrain for Global Capital When Local Housing Becomes an Electronic Instrument' In: Albers, M. B. (ed.) The Political Economy of Mortgage Markets, First Edition, Blackwell Publishing Ltd

Schubert, K. et al. (2009). The Handbook of European Welfare Systems. Abingdon: Routledge

Scruggs, L., & Allan, J. P. (2006a). Welfare-state decommodification in 18 OECD countries: A replication and revision. Journal of European Social Policy, 16, 55–73

Scruggs, L., & Allan, J. P. (2006b). Social Stratification and Welfare Regimes for the 21st Century: Revisiting the "Three Worlds of Welfare Capitalism", Paper prepared for delivery at the 15th International Conference of Europeanists, Drake Hotel, Chicago, IL, March 30-April 1, 2006

Scruggs, L., & Allan, J. P. (2008). "Social Stratification and Welfare Regimes for the Twenty-first Century: Revisiting The Three Worlds of Welfare Capitalism." World Politics 60(4): 642-664

Sharkh, M. A.; Gough, I. (2010). Global Welfare Regimes: A Cluster Analysis. In: Global Social Policy 10(1): 27-58

Sivesind, K. H., Saglie, J. (eds.) 2017. Promoting Active Citizenship Markets and Choice in Scandinavian Welfare. Cham, Switzerland: Palgrave Macmillan

Skocpol, Theda (1995). Social Policy in the United States: Future Possibilities in Historical Perspective. Princeton, New Jersey: Princeton University Press

Smith, K. B. (2002) Typologies, taxonomies, and the benefits of policy classification, Policy Studies Journal, September

Spicker, P. (2014). Social Policy - Theory and Practice. Bristol: Policy Press

Steinmo, S. et al. (1992). Structuring politics: historical institutionalism in comparative analysis. Cambridge University Press, Cambridge [England]; New York

Steinmo, S. (2008). 'What is Historical Institutionalism?' In Donatella Della Porta and Michael Keating (eds), Approaches and Methodologies in the Social Sciences. Cambridge: Cambridge University Press, pp. 150-178

Szelenyi, I., Eyal, G., Townsley, E. (1997). The theory of post-communist managerialism. New Left Review, 1/222

Sydow, J., G. Schreyögg, and J. Koch. 2009. 'Organisational Path Dependence: Opening the Black Box.' Academy of Management Review 34(4): 689–709

Takegawa, S. (2009) 'International circumstances as factors in building a welfare state: welfare regimes in Europe, Japan and Korea', International Journal of Japanese Sociology, 18, 1, 79–96

Taylor-Gooby, P. (1996). The Response of Government: Fragile Convergence? In: Vic George/Peter Taylor-Gooby (Eds.) European Welfare Policy. Squaring the Welfare Circle; Houndmills et. al.: Macmillan Press Ltd., p. 199

Thelen, K. (1999). Historical Institutionalism in Comparative Politics. Annual Review of Political Science 2:1, 369-404

Therborn, G. (2003). Entangled Modernities. In: European Journal of Social Theory 6(3):293–305, http://www.arabphilosophers.com/English/research/nonarabic/Western Modernity/Goran%20Therborn/Entangled_Modernities.pdf

Titmuss, R.M., 1974. Social Policy. George Allen and Unwin, London

Tomka, B. (2006). East Central Europe and the European social policy model: a long-term view. In: East European Review

UNCTAD (2018). Economic Development in Africa Report 2018 Migration for Structural Transformation - Chapter 2: Patterns and trends of migration, Source: https://unctad.org/en/PublicationChapters/edar2018_ch2_en.pdf

Uprety, Dambar and Sylvester, Kevin (2017). The effect of remittances upon skilled emigration: An empirical study, Journal of Economic Development, 42(2)

Van Hear, Nicholas; Bakewell, Oliver and Long, Katy (2012). Drivers of Migration. Migrating out of Poverty – Research Programme Consortium

Van Loon, J., Aalbers, M. B. (2017). How real estate became 'just another asset class': the financialization of the investment strategies of Dutch institutional investors,European Planning Studies, 25:2, 221-240

Voinea, C. F. (2017). On the Elites in the Eastern European Post-Communist Countries Political Elites in the Eastern European Political Regimes After the Fall of the Berlin Wall: An Interdisciplinary Methodological Approach. Conference paper, ECPR General Conference in Oslo, Norway, 6 – 9 September 2017, https://ecpr.eu/ Filestore/PaperProposal/ef9a26b1-15b4-4a98-9b0d-915d696d6cc7.pdf [05.08.2019]

Walker, A. and Wong, C. (2013) 'The ethnocentric construction of the welfare state', in P. Kennett (ed.), A Handbook of Comparative Social Policy, Cheltenham: Edward Elgar

Wallerstein, I. (1984). The politics of the World-Economy: The States, the Movements and the Civilizations. Cambridge: Press Syndicate of the

University of Cambridge Wallerstein, I. (1996). The ANC and South Africa: The Past and Future of Liberation Movements in the World-System. In: Economic and Political Weekly, 31 (39): 2695- 2699

Wallerstein, I. (1999). The End of the World as We Know It Social Science for the Twenty-First Century. Minneapolis: University of Minnesota Press

Wallerstein, I. (2008). The Depression: A Long-Term View. Fernand Braudel Center, Binghamton University, https://www.iwallerstein.com/the-depression-a-long-term- view/ [14.10.2019]

Wallerstein, I. (2011, Jan). The Global Economy Won't Recover, Now or Ever. Foreign Policy, 76. https://manchester.idm.oclc.org/login?url=https://search-proquest-com. manchester.idm.oclc.org/docview/840433861?accountid=12253 [14.10.2019]

Weber, M. (1922). Objectivity in the Theory of Social Sciences and of Social Policy, in Max, Weber, Gesammelte Aufsaetze zur Wissenschaftslehre. Tuebingen: J. C. B., Mohr

Weber, M. (2010). The Protestant Ethnic and the Spirit of Capitalism. Oxford: Oxford University Press

Wilensky, H., 1975. The Welfare State and Equality: Structural and Ideological Roots of Public Expenditures. University of California Press

Wittenberg, J. (2015). Conceptualizing Historical Legacies. In: East European Politics and Societies and Cultures, 29(2): 366-378

Wood, G. and Gough, I. (2006). A comparative welfare regime approach to global social policy. World development, 34 (10): 1696-1712

Zamfir, C. (2013). 'Societatea bună' o nouă provocare pentru sociologie ('The Good Society' a New Challenge for Sociology). Sociologie Românească (Romanian Sociology Journal), 11(4): 3-6

Zolberg, Aristide (1981). "Origins of the Modern World System: A Missing Link", World Politics, vol. 33, no. 2., pp. 253-281

Zolberg, A. (1981) International Migration in Political Perspective. In: Kritz, M., et al., Eds., Global Trends in Migrations: Theory and Research on International Population Movements, Center for Migration Studies Staten Islands, New York, 3-27

Žukowski, M. (2009). Social Regimes in the European Countries, In: Golinowska, S., P. Hengstenberg, and M. Žukowski (eds.), Diversity and Commonality in European Social Policies: The Forging of a European Social Model (Warszaw: Scholar)

Index of terms

Lightning Source UK Ltd.
Milton Keynes UK
UKHW021832231120
373958UK00003B/61